MORE GHOST TRAILS OF NORTHUMBRIA

by
Clive Kristen

Casdec Ltd

Dedication

To Duncan Elson and Mark Nuttall
for making me look good.

Published by Casdec Ltd
22 Harraton Terrace
Birtley
Chester-le-Street
Co. Durham
DH3 2QG

Tel: (091) 410 5556
Fax: (091) 410 0229

Written by Clive Kristen

First Published May 1993

ISBN - 0 907595 85 5

The Ancient Brinkburn Priory

Author's Note

Dear Ghosthunter,

This book is a companion volume to Ghost Trails of Northumbria. It contains five new 'tour and explore' trails linked by supernatural themes

These trails have been constructed to take best advantage of the great natural beauty of the region, and to bring to life Northumbria's rich historical and cultural heritage.

The 'touring times' suggested for each trail are based on a fairly brisk schedule. For those who prefer relaxed ghosthunting each trail can be conveniently broken down into sections. The Trail Guides provided with each section are intended only to help make sense of the text. They are not to scale and should not be regarded as an adequate substitute for a good map.

Whist every effort has been made to produce accurate historical and topographical detail, the reader will understand that no area of human consciousness is more prone to misinterpretation, confusion, and even dishonesty than the supernatural.

In an attempt to make sense of this dilemma the book tries to balance traditional accounts of supernatural phenomena, archive and historical material with the common sense of local knowledge. When it has been necessary to select one version of a story from several, contemporary and local accounts have taken precedence.

The historical notes are intended to fill out detail where it has not been appropriate to do so within the main body the text. This final section also corrects a measure of imbalance. It was impossible to discuss the Bamburgh area without referring in some detail to two great Northumberland heroines - Grace Darling and Dorothy Forster. But Sir John Forster - the Robert Maxwell of the 16th. century - is mentioned all too briefly. In many ways he is a more significant historical figure and a most celebrated ghost.

I am indebted to archivists and librarians in Britain and abroad without whose patience and perseverance this would have been a very much slimmer volume. I also extend grateful thanks to my wife, Maureen, for her encouragement, ghosthunting and mapmaking skills. Finally I thank all the people who have given me primary source material for this book by telling their tales of encounters with the supernatural.

Clive Kristen
March 1993

The Writer

Former teacher and lecturer, CLIVE KRISTEN, joined the ranks of professional writers four years ago.

He had previously achieved some notoriety as the creator of the popular folk song THE PHANTOM FLASHER. His ambition is to write the kind of filmscripts that force him to work with beautiful women in exotic locations.

Clive is a regular contributor to a number of national publications which include LE MAGAZINE and FOOTBALL MONTHLY. He is best known in the region as an outspoken freelance news and feature writer for the NORTHUMBERLAND GAZETTE.

In addition to the best selling GHOST TRAILS OF NORTHUMBRIA, another companion volume to this title - MURDER AND MYSTERY TRAILS OF NORTHUMBRIA - has been inflicted on the world at the same time. The author has also recently completed 'VENTURES INTO EUROPE', a HOW TO guide, offering independent advice to those considering the purchase of property in France. A first novel, FROST AND FIRE, is in preparation.

The Photographer

DUNCAN ELSON is well established as one of the region's leading portrait and landscape photographers. His atmospheric photography for GHOST TRAILS OF NORTHUMBRIA has been matched in this latest volume. Duncan has also contributed the pictures to the third CASDEC book in the series - MURDER AND MYSTERY TRAILS OF NORTHUMBRIA. He is now working with the writer on a new project, COQUETDALE NOW AND THEN, which he modestly describes as ' the definitive photographic gallery of Northumbria's most beautiful valley.'

Duncan's ambition is to see his name in the GUINNESS BOOK Of RECORDS as the organiser of the WORLD'S BIGGEST FLASH. This will bring together thousands of sponsored photographers who will take a simultaneous night exposure of Rothbury village.

Duncan's award winning work has qualified him as a Master Photographer and he is a Licentiate Member of the British Institute of Professional Photographers.

The Illustrator

The cover and map designs again show two creative facets in the wide repertoire of MARK NUTTALL's skills as an illustrator. His cover for the first GHOST TRAILS book was considered to be an important reason for the impact of the book. Certainly it was eye catching. The National Trust refused to continue to stock the volume, despite a useful sales record, because Mark's design was too lurid for the sensitivities of National Trust visitors. Such a recommendation made it certain that Mark would be invited to illustrate the companion volumes.

Together with the author Mark created RAMBO THE GIANT FERRET. First featured in newsprint on April 1st. 1989, RAMBO has passed into local folklore as the scourge of Coquetdale.

Mark, who is currently working in graphic design for television, is also noted for his distinctive cartoon strips. He is presently illustrating a book of anecdotes provided by the rich and famous. His ambition is to become equally rich and famous.

Tynan Weir
March 1993.

Contents

Taking Care in the Countryside

Most of the sites in this book can be accessed from public rights of way. Where this does not happen visitors can get a good impression of a site from suggested viewpoints.

Much of the land is farmed, and should be treated with respect. In a few cases, access is restricted and the necessary consents should be obtained. Special care is required during the lambing season and visitors are requested to follow the guidelines of the country code. Please follow footpaths, close gates, and keep dogs under close control. Litter is unsightly and can cause injury and suffering to animals.

Some of the buildings mentioned are private homes. Please do not trespass or behave intrusively. Property owners have been generous in the information they have provided. Please ensure that their right to quiet and privacy is preserved.

These tours are designed for the motorist and none of the walks suggested are arduous. Nevertheless, Northumbrian weather can be unpredictable - even in summer. It is suggested that visitors do not set out on a walk alone. They should have adequate footwear and a waterproof garment. A good map and compass are also highly recommended.

The Author

Author, Clive Kristen

Through The Eye Of The Camera

When it comes to ghosts, I'm not sure. Most religions share the belief that we have a spirit that continues to exist after our death. It seems fair enough then to assume that every now and again those spirits will continue an earthly vigil rather than beginning their journey elsewhere.

Taking photographs for the Ghost Trails books has been a fascinating experience. No, I have not seen or photographed a single ghost, but on several occasions I did sense they were there.

I'm also sure they have a sense of humour. Following the trails I've had far more than the usual quota of things going wrong. Batteries that had just been replaced would die. Filters I'm sure I'd packed would temporarily vanish, only to turn up later when I didn't need them. On more than one occasion the lens jammed altogether and I had to use a backup camera.

Most of the pictures were taken during February and March, so I visited a lot of places that were cold and empty. But many times I felt the level of chill had little to do with the weather.

During the winter months when the stone is cold, the light grey and the landscape bleak, it is easy to feel of days of BC - Before (Micro) Chip - when all man had to communicate with was his senses. At these times you understand best the meaning of 'living stone'. Sometimes you can imagine that the whole landscape is trying to say something to you.

These stories bring the past to life in a way that no history lesson can. They capture the mood of the past as much as the people and places.

Trailers who seek to capture their own photographic record should use the widest angles possible. It is the best way to capture to mood, power, and great beauty of the Northumbrian landscape.

Figures are useful for giving a scale and perspective, but it is generally best to shoot your family and friends from as close as possible. Their features then become an important part of the picture. Or, as they believe in some of the world's less sophisticated societies, you are perhaps capturing something of their spirit on film.

I hope you enjoy this second collection of trails as much as I have.

Duncan Elson. (Master Photographer)
Rothbury. April 1993.

The Region's Top Prize Winning Photographer - Duncan Elson

No. 1
The
Cheby
Chase

This linear motoring tour takes about four hours

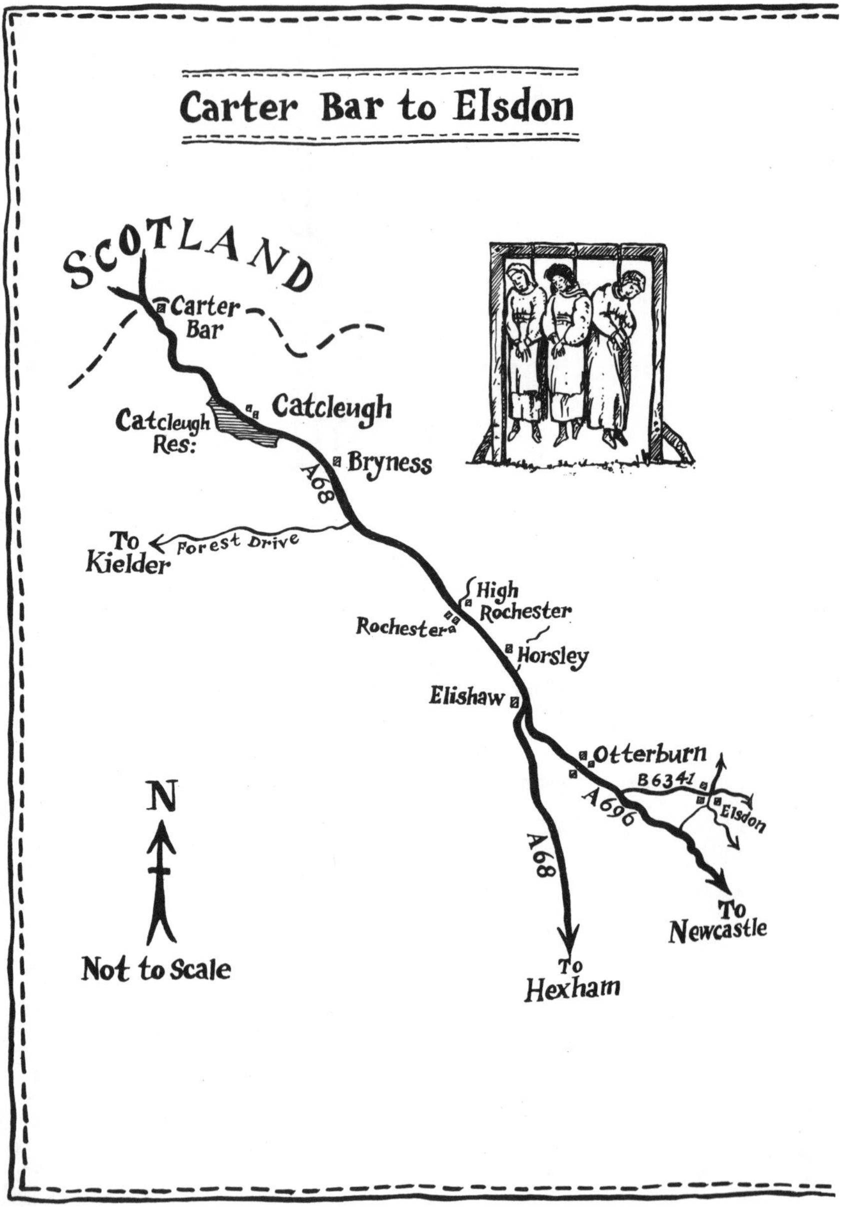

Carter Bar to Elsdon

SCOTLAND

Carter Bar

Catcleugh Res:

Catcleugh

A68

Bryness

To Kielder

Forest Drive

High Rochester

Rochester

Horsley

Elishaw

Otterburn

B6341

A696

Elsdon

A68

N

Not to Scale

To Hexham

To Newcastle

Border Country

Carter Bar is the classic border crossing. From this vantage point high in the Cheviots the forests and hills of Northumberland and Roxburghshire spread out like spokes on a wheel. To the south is Kielder and Redesdale. To the west is Wauchope. To the north the road falls gently to the famous border town of Jedburgh.

30 miles south of England's most northerly town, Berwick, this crossing is a dramatic and forbidding landscape of no man's land.The line runs as much south as west. Here is a natural frontier created along a line of hills. It's often bleak in summer and impassable in winter : most of the inhabitants have woollen coats and four legs

The Chevy Chase

The first public transport system in the area was a coach, called the Chevy Chase, that ran from Carter Bar to Elsdon. This is also the route followed by the trail.

The Reivers

The reivers were notorious 'names' from both sides of the border. Whilst agriculture was the principle occupation, the reivers (or Moss Troopers) supplemented their income by stealing cattle. The more successful 'names' added kidnapping and extortion to their profit ledgers. Arson, rape and murder were a matter of routine.

Blood feuds developed from the middle ages onwards. By the close of the 16th. century revenge motivated attacks as much as profit. The union of crowns in 1603 was the beginning of the end for the reivers.

But border families have long memories. The last full scale raid was in 1715 when two groups of 'names' combined to take advantage of the distraction of the Jacobite invasion. The moss trooping era ended perhaps with a number of arrests and summary executions a few years later. However, certain cross border rugby fixtures, and the odd incident at village dances, remind us that the reiver spirit is alive and kicking today.

Sir John Forster

Sir John Forster was the Robert Maxwell of the 16th. century. The only blemish on an otherwise distinguished career of villainy occurred near Carter Bar.

Sir John was the first great name of the Bamburgh dynasty of Forsters. If his story isn't quite ' rags to riches' it's near enough to make it fascinating.

As the second son of a not particularly wealthy father life was not too promising. But young John Forster was determined to climb to the top. He served Henry VIII loyally and was well rewarded. He was shrewd enough to marry a beautiful Blanchland heiress. Whilst still a young man he paid £650 - the equivalent perhaps of a million today - for his lands. By now he was Lord Constable of Bamburgh, Warden of the Middle Marches and one of the most powerful landowners in Northumbria. His considerable rent revenues were topped up by stripping castles, dodgy dealings, and hugely profitable border raids. His income was considerable, but his expenses (which included maintaining ever increasing numbers of illegitimate children and several legal heirs) meant his villainy had to be as constant as one of the most colourful characters in Northumbria's history. His most famous gesture was delayed. Despite his legendary capacity for strong ale and sustained debauchery, Sir John lived to 101 years of age. This makes it difficult perhaps to accuse him of dissolute lifestyle.

If Sir John wasn't exactly a role model, he was certainly a source of inspiration and encouragement to future generations of the region's villains.

The Reidswire Raid

Sir John's one serious blunder was the Reidswire Raid. This occurred close to Carter Bar on what was supposed to be a regular truce day.

The idea was that the Warden of the Middle Marches should have regular contact with his 'opposite number'. This was Sir John Carmichael, the Scottish Warden. The truce was an opportunity to exchange prisoners and information.

Sir John had promised to produce a notorious villain - a member of the Charleton family. He made excuses. First he said he'd failed to apprehend the man. When this was disproved, he claimed the prisoner had escaped.

The Scottish Warden was angry. It was clear to him that Sir John was shielding the man for his own purposes. Carmichael told Sir John a few home truths. Sir John became abusive and drew his sword. A skirmish followed.

Sir John's temper had overcome his common sense. It the only time in his life that he failed to measure the strength of the opposition. In a brief but furious fight he was bundled from his horse. Carmichael must have considered striking a fatal blow, but perhaps he assessed that the repercussions would be too great. Instead, Sir John was trussed like a chicken, thrown in a cart, and taken to the Scottish Regent in Edinburgh. A few days later he was released and sent home with placatory presents.

Such was the meaning of fear and power four centuries ago.

The Leap Hill Phantom

Less fortunate in the skirmish was young Thomas Ellesden. He loyally rode to the rescue of Sir John only to be intercepted by two Scottish veterans. His armour was scant protection against the force of the claymore. His helmet was removed by the first blow and his head with the second.

The site of the skirmish is about half a mile east along the border line from Carter Bar close to the summit of Leap Hill. There's a tradition of hearing the sounds of battle around this spot. Local farmers dismiss the noise as the roaring of the wind around the peaks.

But the spectre of Thomas Ellesden is more difficult to explain. It has been witnessed dozens of times. Perhaps the most vivid and recent account comes from Brian Osborne of Kelso.

The Hiker's Tale

" Jan (my girlfriend) and I were walking the ridge in 1987. We were just above the Leithope Forest. "

" We sat on the grass. The view was fabulous. It was the middle of a summer's day in July. There was hardly any breeze so we were sitting on our cagoules. It was the kind of day when you could easily doze off in the sunshine. "

" I thought I heard someone coming up behind us, but when I turned there was nothing there. Jan must have heard it. She looked round just after me. "

" I heard her screaming and saw her point. I turned round again. There was a man standing about fifty yards away. His back was towards us. You could see armour shining in the sun. "

" I thought that someone must be filming, but there was nobody else around. Jan was still screaming. I jumped up and looked hard at the man. He seemed odd, but somehow I didn't at first realise what was wrong. I must have been so frightened and confused my brain just wasn't accepting the evidence of my eyes. Slowly he began to move away down the hillside. It was only then that I took it in. There was the jagged shape of a neck but no head."

" I couldn't hear Jan any more. My eyes seemed stuck on him. As he went down the hill the body began to disappear. The last thing I saw was the neck. It was higher on one side than the other. "

" After he went I heard Jan sobbing. I put my arm around her. It was some time before either of us were in any kind of control. We put our cagoules on because we were cold. I won't forget that feeling of cold. The ends of my fingers were numb. Freezing numb with cold in the middle of summer. I'll never go near that terrible place again. "

Catcleugh

The road is lined with larches as you approach the dam at Catcleugh. The view back into the Cheviots is impressive with White Crag and Carter Fell as the most prominent features.

In the grounds of Catcleugh below there is a wooden hut. It is 100 years old. This is the token survivor of 47 'cottages' built for the workers who created the reservoir. Close to the peak of the project, in 1888, there were 331 men, 70 women, and 94 children living in the huts.

The one survivor was last occupied by a family called Milburn. Like the others it became deserted when the work on the reservoir was complete. Most were quickly demolished. This one was useful for a while as a tool store and office. It was finally left to rot in the 1930s. Though in poor condition, the last hut was rescued and restored by the National Park. It is preserved as a small, but important insight into Northumbrian history.

A Wandering Spirit

The most famous phantom of these parts is the celebrated ghost of Percy Reed.

Popular Percy - the Keeper of Redesdale - was invited on a hunt by members of the Hall family. They were jealous of his office and the enormous respect he'd won locally.

The hunt took place alongside a stream, variously described as the Glen of Bateinghope and the Chattelhope Burn. The Halls chose their moment to murder

Catcleugh

an unarmed man. Tradition has it that four stab wounds were inflicted - one by each of 'the false hearted Halls.'

Percy's haunting zone is extensive. There have been sightings along the banks of the Rede between Todlawhaugh and Pringlehaugh. His favourite haunt was once said to be around Todlaw Mill. There is uncertainty about the exact site of the mill. It's likely to have disappeared, but there are suggestions that it could be the wood mill at Stobbs.

The ghost is said to be a benign spirit that has rescued many travellers lost in poor weather. The apparition wears a distinctive hunting green.

Robin Of Redesdale

The hunting green is also associated with Robin Hood. A number of eminent historians have forged connections between Robin and Redesdale.

Although legend links the fortunes of Robin Hood with Sherwood and Nottingham, it is likely that the merry men were itinerants who found a safe haven in several of the great English forests.

At the end of the 12th. century King Richard's England was massively forested. The Lion Heart himself scarcely visited these shores and left the country under the control of his barons. The barons were almost kings in their own district. An outlaw from one area would seek sanctuary in another. It was not unknown for a baron to welcome outlaws for their nuisance value against a rival. The more prudent outlaws were aware that circumstances could change quickly. Nuisances were negotiable currency in the Middle Ages. Outlaws rarely outstayed their welcome.

The legend was created by ballads. The earliest mention of the name is in Piers Plowman (c. 1377). This links Robin Hood with ' Randolf', Earl of Chester. 'Randolf' is said to be Randle, the third Earl, who flourished during the reigns of Richard I, John and Henry III. He held property and hunting rights in Redesdale.

The second document to mention the name is Andrew of Wynstoun's Chronicle of Scotland (c. 1420). Here both Robin Hood and Little John are placed in Barnysdale or Barnessdale. There are at least two Northumbrian possibilities here. One is the area of upper Teesdale north of Barnard Castle. The other is around Byrness, or the northern fringe of the Redesdale Forest. A ballad written a few years later (c. 1435) puts Robin at Garreysgyll. This may well be Garrisgill, near Alston.

There is equally compelling evidence to place Robin Hood in South Yorkshire and Nottinghamshire, but Northumbria can stake a fair claim. But is the Sherwood connection more likely?

Sherwood Forest is not mentioned in the earliest ballads. We must rely on finding the Barnsdale of Wynstoun's Chronicle. By far the most likely candidate is the Barnsdale situated between Doncaster and Nottingham - once the heart of the greenwood area.

There is also the Robert of Locksley connection. Locksley - sometimes said to be Robin Hood - was a 'manslayer from Bradfield in Hallamshire'. The 'fair town of Locksley' has been searched for by academics without convincing success. Equally confusing is the large number of Bradfields. Only Hallamshire provides a strong clue. Robin of Locksley almost certainly came from the Sheffield area to the west of Sherwood Forest.

Was it Robin of Redesdale or Robin of Sherwood? It could easily be both. The chances are that Robin Hood, an itinerant outlaw, travelled widely throughout the north country. Some suggest that the many places associated with his name prove the case. Others point out that this has probably more to do with the enduring popularity of the legend.

During the reign of King John a number of outlaw bands became established in the border region. One reason for this was the lawlessness of the area. This lack of law and order was a big bonus in the outlaw business.

The late 12th. century was the beginning of the age of the reivers. Is it just possible that Robin Hood was one of them?

Robin's Resting Place

As Robin Hood lay dying from poison we are told that he fired an arrow into the air. Where it landed was the place he was to be buried.

A grave in the garden of a private house in Redesdale has been claimed as that of England's best known folk hero. It is a quiet place surrounded by mature trees. Best to leave it undisturbed.

The True Cost Of Water

Byrness claims to be the last village in England. It was once a very scattered community but most of the population now live in the forestry village.

Just below Byrness is the tiny Church of Saint Francis. It was built in 1786 mainly to serve as a chapel of rest. Later it became a parish church and a small school was attached to it. It is now mainly noted for its stained glass window - a poignant memorial to those who lost their lives in the construction of the Catcleugh reservoir.

There is a car parking area below the church. A key to the building is available from the petrol station nearby.

The Church of St. Francis, Byrness

64 people died between 1891 and 1904 - the years of construction. 15 of those killed were women. The Reverend Roberts lost his life in a freak accident in 1902. All this represents more than four fatalities a year, a true measure perhaps of the true cost of water. Almost all those who worked on the reservoir were recruited from Tyneside.

They Also Served

There is another unusual monument in the church. It is a First World War memorial that lists the name of women who also served.

The monument is important. It proves that women in a rural community were publicly acknowledged long before this happened in most towns. It almost challenges the concept of the countryside as the last bastion of chauvinism.

Perhaps it is not so surprising. An early Victorian writer put it like this : ' Redesdale is no place for a delicate constitution or the affectations of the city. The womenfolk work alongside the men. In former times they knew as much of the art of the sword as the quilting pin. '

George Carr

A small iron cross under an alder tree in the churchyard speaks the last word about the nature of this community.

Memorial to George Carr, aged 11.

The inscription reads : 'In memory of George Carr. Accidentally killed at Catcleugh, June 15th.1901. Erected by his teachers and schoolfellows.'

Little John's Waterfall

The forest drive turns sharply off the A68 below Byrness. Just before the toll, turn left to Blakehopeburnhaugh car park. The laid out circular forest walk takes about half an hour and is well worth it.

The main focus of the walk is a waterfall. This has been associated with water sprites - a mischievous gang of forest fairies who take delight in unbalancing walkers and pitching them into the water. Those who try to walk behind the falls will almost certainly find that the sprites give them a soaking.

The Blakehopeburn is noted for another encounter. Is this not the very place where Robin of Redesdale first met Little John? The quarterstaff battle that followed was a clear points win for the larger man. It is only fair then that the waterfall should be named after him

By The Roaring River

The Roman stronghold of Bremenium can be found by turning up a side road to the left a mile after the village of Rochester. The turning is by the speed deregulation sign.

High Rochester is a short way up the hillside. It is no more than a couple of farmhouses and a village green. This green was once the heart of Bremenium, which means 'place by the roaring river.'

You need a trained eye to see anything very Roman today. Careful observation is rewarded by identifying fragments of walls and towers. Best preserved is a relative term here. The most obvious feature though are the remains of the west gateway and part of the surrounding wall.

In its heyday, around the year 300 AD, Bremenium held a garrison of trained infantry and cavalry. There is evidence too of the Romans high tech weapon - the ballistae. This was a spring loaded device that could throw lumps of stone huge distances. Two of the stone balls can be seen at the old village schoolhouse.

The Furthest Frontier

The Romans built the first Bremenium around AD 80. As a fortified stronghold it lasted for almost three hundred years.

A whole Roman legion was wiped out on a disastrous patrol not many miles from here. It was enough to encourage the Emperor Hadrian to bring forward his plans of wall building. At a later date Bremenium was a staging post for the second wall - the Antonine - which ran from the Firth of Forth to the Clyde. It was after the Antonine was breached and abandoned in AD 196 that Bremenium became the northernmost outpost of Rome.

During its turbulent history Bremenium was sacked and rebuilt at least three times. The 'Barbarian Conspiracy' of AD 367 was the beginning of the end. Within three years Roman Britain had vanished for ever.

The Barefoot Woman

With so much macho activity it is perhaps odd to note that the phantom associated with Bremenium is a woman.

A barefoot and scantily clad lady has been seen close to the west gate remains. The time is invariably high summer around sunset. She sits and she weeps. Sometimes she is heard to call out the name 'Drusus'.

The suggestion is that the unnamed and unhappy spectre awaits the return of her legionary lover. We will never know for sure. She vanishes before anyone can come close enough to ask.

The Horsley Connection

A little further down the A68 is the village of Horsley. The Victorian Holy Trinity Church is an austere building to the left of the main road.

The steep path to the church doorway can be dangerous in wet or frosty weather. In Redesdale this means that care should be taken on most days of the year. In the church porch there is a Roman altar found at the nearby Featherwood fort

The view over the Rede valley from this point is excellent. The wooded area across the river contains the remains of a deserted medieval village.

First And Last Chance

The Redesdale Arms is an excellent hostelry at which to break the journey. It is open all day. Even better, they seem to serve food here at all hours.

This was once the 'First and Last' house. Travelling south this was once the first inn in England. The title has been recently stolen by a modern hostelry further north. But don't be confused. The Redesdale Arms is the real thing : every inch a fine old English inn. To most people it will always be the authentic 'First and Last.'

The inn is based on a 14th. century fortified farmhouse - or bastle. The animals slept below and the people above. Some locals will tell you that very little has

The Original & Best First & Last Inn

changed over the years.The oldest stones of the existing building can be seen at the foot of the wall near the car park area.

The Warriors' Seat

On the north side of the A68 at Bennetsfield there is an unusual, large Victorian stone seat.

It is a reminder of the courage of the leading protagonists of the Battle of Otterburn - Harry Percy and the Earl of Douglas.

The date of the battle is given on one of the panels as 12th. August 1388. Harry Percy, who earned the name 'Hotspur' because he was ever anxious to join in a fight, was perhaps delayed - just this once. The battle was fought three days later on August 15th.

The battle was little more than a regular border skirmish. However, Harry

The Warrior's Seat

Hotspur was both the most outrageously brave and boneheaded of the Percys. This fairly insignificant event has therefore held constant appeal to songsters and poets.

Two of the inscriptions on the Bennetsfied seat are the words of famous writers :

' Give me the making of the people's songs and I will let who will make their laws.' *Andrew Fletcher.*

" I never hear the old song of Percy and Douglas that found not my heart more moved than with a trumpet.' *Sir Philip Sidney.*

The first inscription is a nugget of 18th. century Scottish wisdom. It is an epigram on the social impact of literature. The second, penned two centuries earlier, makes much the same point.

The Percy Stone

Turning left on the A696 brings you to the traditional site of the battle. The stone which marks the spot is a late 18th. century replacement for an earlier one that had disappeared. Those who placed the 'Percy Cross' here got the right date but the wrong place. The conflict was centred on a strip of land half a mile away towards Otterburn Hall.

Although the Scots were victorious in the battle, it was their leader who was killed. It is typical of Northumbrians that the stone should commemorate not a victory, but a glorious defeat.

There has been another suggestion. Could the stone mark the place where the funeral procession of the Earl of Douglas began?

It was a medieval custom to erect a cross marking the place where the coffin of a important person rested each night on its homeward journey. Douglas's body was taken over the Cheviot hills to Melrose Abbey. A line of markings - called the Golden Pots - runs in that direction from the Percy Stone.

Battle Stone, Otterburn

Unfortunately, historical evidence suggests these are more likely to be Roman markers along Dere Street.

The Hotspur Mythology

The Battle of Otterburn, also called Chevy Chase, was intended as revenge for the Percys on the Earl of Douglas who had successfully ravaged Northumbria.

Harry Hotspur had followed Douglas from Newcastle. Douglas was unconcerned about the small Percy army and was happy to wait for them to turn up at Otterburn.

It was late in the day when Harry Percy and his brother Ralph arrived. Convention had it that battle would commence the following morning at a mutually convenient time.

Although the Percy force was weary from marching, Harry Hotspur was determined to take the initiative. He attacked by moonlight.

The element of surprise could have helped. But Harry Hotspur was a traditionalist. He announced himself with the customary trumpet calls and battle cries. His key weapon - the famous Northumberland archers - was largely wasted. The men were not used to aiming at highly mobile shadowy targets.

The fight soon became a brutal hand to hand affair and the Scots numerical superiority and freshness began to tell. Harry Hotspur ignored the carnage around him and cut his way into the heaviest of the fighting. The tradition is that he personally ran his sword through Earl Douglas. This myth was begun by the chronicler Thomas Walsingham. It was later perpetuated by Raphael Holinshed - Shakespeare's source for Henry IV Part One. The play has itself become an important source, not only of millions of hours of classroom torment, but of the received reputation of Harry Hotspur as a glamorous warrior prince.

In fact this battle ended ignominiously for Harry Percy. When the battle was clearly lost, he tried to escape the field and was taken prisoner by Sir John Montgomery.

The survivors of his force fought rearguard actions as far as Elsdon. They then scattered onto the high moors. Most escaped, but some were rounded up and taken prisoner by the Scots.

Harry Hotspur was later released on the payment of a huge ransom to which King Richard II contributed £3,000.

An Action Replay

There are many reports of ghostly phenomena associated with the battle.

The most enduring is the action replay that was reported in 1888, exactly 500 years after the famous skirmish.

Farmers Percival Hall and John Ellesden were driving sheep close to the battleground area. It was already dusk on a warm August night. First they heard the sound of hoofbeats and trumpets in the distance. Then they saw a column of cavalry gathering on the high ground above them. The column broke into three sections and set off down from the ridge and away from their view.

The men rushed up the incline. It was after sunset now, but a full moon lit the fields below.

Percival Hall said he could make out a shadowy whirling movement of many men fighting below. John Ellesden saw nothing. But both men heard the sound of metal on metal, the frightened whinnying of horses, and the shouts of men in combat.

Home On The Ranges

Otterburn offers an excellent hostelry - the Percy Arms - and several gift shops.

It is a village whose name is still associated with military matters. The biggest local employer is the army who have huge artillery ranges throughout the area.

The statistics are remarkable. Otterburn ranges are the largest single piece of military land in Britain. They cover more than a fifth of the National Park. It's been called a massive self-catering military theme park.

Over 30,000 men come to the ranges to train each year. This represents 300,000 man days of training. Each year there are four million firings, which includes more than 1000 missiles at £8,000 a throw. Opinions of what this represents are seldom moderate. It's either the biggest and most wasteful fireworks party in the UK, or a vital component of the machine that preserves freedom.

There is restricted public access to the ranges which include some of the finest walking country in England. The military have a good relationship with the public. They ask only that you watch out for red flags which mark daily danger zones, keep to the footpaths, and not to take any interesting bits of metal home to play with later.

A Capital Place

Elsdon was once the capital of Redesdale. Today it is a delightful village with most of the houses nestling around a large green. This was once a meeting place for the Redesdale clans and a cattle holding area.

The most notable buildings are St. Cuthbert's Church, the late 14th. century pele tower, and the Bird in the Bush Inn. *

Saint Cuthbert Was Here

The church was built during the early years of the 15th. century on one of the many sites where St. Cuthbert's body rested on its travels. Above the doorway are parts of old grave stones - one carved with a dagger, the other with shears. These are powerful symbols of the history of Elsdon itself : a farming community frequently disturbed by violence. There are churchyard symbols that also reflect the only certainty of our existence : they are the Grim Reaper and the Death's Head.

In 1810 more than 100 skeletons were found tightly packed against the north wall of the church. In 1877 more bones were found in rows that extended from the north wall under the church itself.

St. Cuthbert's Church, Elsdon

Although the present buildings were begun after the Battle of Otterburn it is clear that this was already consecrated ground. It is known that the bodies of many who died in the battle were carried to Elsdon. The church is built over what may well be more mass graves.

Beyond the north wall of the churchyard irregular contours present the possibility of yet more burial grounds. The Victorian historian, Robert Hughill, responded to the drunken taunts of a local farmer by suggesting these could be plague pits

The church itself contains some unusual artifacts.

One is a monumental tablet that was brought from Bremenium in 1809. The Latin inscriptions translate as : ' Julia Lucilla saw this stone was erected to her very meritorious husband, who was an inspector under the surveyor of public works. He lived 47 years, 6 months and 25 days.' There are early medieval tombstones in the north transept. One shows a fine pilgrim's staff and crusader's sword.

At the west end of the church there is a case that contains three horse's skulls. These were found during the spire restoration of 1877. An unlikely suggestion is that they are relics of a pagan custom which featured equine sacrifice.

The Reivers' Revenge

The pele tower was designed to protect the rectors of Elsdon against the unwelcome attentions of the reivers. It was basically a large house designed with extra thick walls, a vaulted ground floor and a roof parapet.

The most serious raid occurred in 1585 when 400 members of the Elliot and Armstrong clans attacked Elsdon. 14 men were killed, 200 prisoners were taken for ransom, and more than 300 oxen and horses were stolen. There was also wholesale looting and the theft of over £500 in cash. As the reivers left the village they threw flaming torches through the open doors and windows.

The raid was said to be in response to representations made to the authorities the previous year by John Hall of Overacres, who claimed that members of the Elliot clan had stolen his animals and murdered members of his family.

Elsdon remained a troubled place to live until the middle of the 17th. century. In 1618 there were still three 'official' Elsdon outlaws - Michael Pott, and Martin and George Hall. Their crimes included horse and sheep stealing.

As late as 1660 there was a serious raid on the rectory. A gang of thieves smashed their way into the building and held the minister, Jeremiah Nelson, at gunpoint. They collected a bag of money and valuables and escaped.

Howdie The Midwife

An odd story associated with Elsdon is that of Howdie the Midwife.   Howdie was woken up one night by a banging on her door. A well dressed messenger asked her to come quickly. The midwife was offered a large sum of money for her services, but she was not to know who the expectant mother was.

The midwife was blindfolded and taken to a cottage somewhere nearby. When the hood was removed she recognised neither the young woman in the bed nor the room itself.

After the baby was delivered, Howdie was given a box of strange smelling ointment by an old woman who appeared to be the young mother's 'nurse'. She was told to put some on the baby's face, but to be careful not to touch her own.

Howdie tried to follow the instruction, but smoke from a candle had irritated her eyes and she rubbed them.

From that moment she remembered nothing until she woke up in a wood with a purse of gold at her side.

A few days later Howdie was shopping at the market when she recognised the old woman who had given her the ointment. She challenged her, and the 'nurse' replied : " Which eye do you see me with? "

Howdie told her the left eye. The old woman came close and spat straight into the midwife's left eye. It burned as if touched by a hot iron. Howdie called for water to ease the sharpness of the pain. Someone drew a tub fresh from the well and Howdie dipped her napkin into it. The burning sensation soon disappeared.

But Howdie was blind in that eye for the rest of her life

Where Is Winter?

Above Elsdon on the Morpeth road is the celebrated Winter's Gibbet.* A mystery remains as to what happened to the body of the notorious murderer that was hung in chains here.

Elsdon Gibbet - A Grim Reminder

By tradition the bones are buried beneath the gibbet. But it is known that at least part of the pathetic remains were removed by ghoulish trophy hunters, and it has been suggested that some local people felt things had gone far enough.

It is probable that the body was removed quietly and buried somewhere nearby. It may be significant that most of the sightings of Winter's ghost occur not at the gibbet itself, but close to the woods near the cattle grid. This point is around 100 metres from the gibbet.

Brown Man Or Deugar?

Another strange story is linked with this high point of the moors. On an autumn day In 1714 two Newcastle men had been shooting game. They were sitting by a small stream counting their 'bag' when they were approached by a stunted hunchback who wore a long brown cloak.

The dwarf muttered some odd words that the men did not understand, but they could tell by his tone that he was angry. They offered to give him the game but he shook his head. The dwarf emptied his pockets to show that he ate only berries and fruit. He beckoned with his hand for them to follow him.

The men were not sure what they should do. There was something very odd about the stranger that went beyond his strange speech and appearance. They argued with each other about what they should do. They finally decided to follow the dwarf, but when they turned round he had vanished.

The dwarf in this story bears a strong resemblance to two characters that occur elsewhere in popular Northumbrian folklore. The first is the Deugar*, associated with the Simonside ridge, not many miles from here. The main physical characteristics are similar. The Deugar is an anti-social mini-hunchback who speaks mainly halitosis. His favourite occupation is luring walkers to their doom and roasting their corpses gently over a peat fire.

The other is the Brown Man of the Moors, a vegetarian mini-mystic who predicted great danger for the Lord of Kielder if he accepted Lord Soulis's dinner invitation.**

It is possible that we are looking at a spider's web of related legends based around the same character. But there are differences. The Deugar is at best a part time vegetarian.

The mysterious and evil dwarf is an enduring character in British and European folklore. Perhaps one day someone will publish a thesis on the subject. Until then, the reader may choose any theory he likes about connections or otherwise between devious dwarfs, Brown Men and Deugars.

* This story featured in Ghost Trails of Northumbria.

** This story featured in Murder and Mystery Trails of Northumbria.

No. 2
The
Magic
Kingdom

This linear walking and motoring tour
takes approximately seven hours

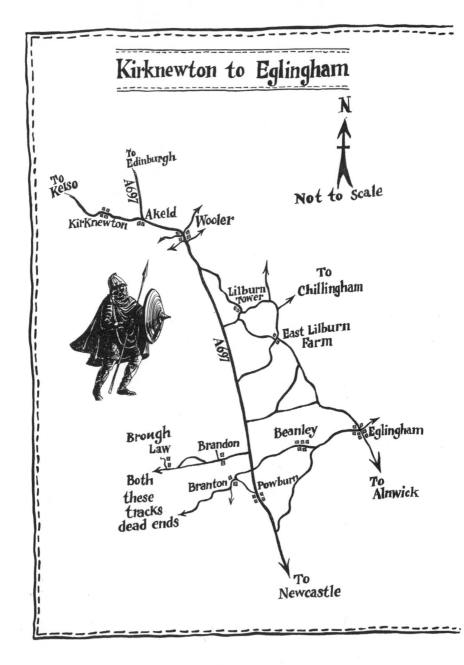

Kirknewton to Eglingham

N

Not to Scale

To Edinburgh

To Kelso

A697

Kirknewton

Akeld

Wooler

Lilburn Tower

To Chillingham

A697

East Lilburn Farm

Brough Law

Brandon

Beanley

Eglingham

Both these tracks dead ends

Branton

Powburn

To Alnwick

To Newcastle

Wild Country

There is no true wilderness. Even in the remotest areas of Northumbria you still see a landscape shaped by man. But this trail takes in some of the wildest and most beautiful countryside in England. The three walk options are not arduous but they are in countryside where you may not see another living soul. It is important to have strong footwear, a good waterproof layer, and a map and compass. You are strongly advised not to walk alone.

Where Waters Meet

Kirknewton, at the junction of the College Burn and River Glen is today little more than a hamlet. It was once a small border town. The thick walls of the buildings indicate its troubled past.

The church dates from Saxon times and may well have been a place of worship throughout the Christian era.

The Church of the Kilted Magi

Near the churchyard entrance, close to the waters of a small burn, there are lonely rows of graves signalling the last resting place of young pilots killed in training missions in 1943 and 1944.

What The Butler Saw

To the west of the tower there is the grave of Josephine Butler.

She was a leading Victorian social reformer who helped to change attitudes to women and to generally improve their lot. She demanded and won improvements in workhouse conditions. Josephine saw for herself the plight of women in garrison towns and ports. After working amongst the prostitutes of Liverpool, she led a 20 year campaign against the Contagious Diseases Act. This was an instrument of law which forced women to join an official register in order to continue their trade. The law also gave police the power to arrest suspected women and to have them medically examined and forcibly treated. It was largely through Josephine's influence that the Act was suspended in 1883 and abolished three years later.

Josephine tackled many other institutional double standards of the day. She was also outspoken in her demands for various causes of liberty. These included women's rights and the freedom of the individual. It is often said it was Josephine Butler who laid the foundations for what later became the suffragette movement.

The Kilted Magi

Inside the church there is a carving thought to be Saxon in origin. It features the Virgin and the Three Wise Men. These gentlemen appear to be wearing skirts and the carving has become popularly known as The Kilted Magi.

The Walls Of Gefrin

An unusual monument on the brow of a hill on the B6531 marks the site of the Saxon township of Gefrin. There is absolutely nothing more to see today, but excavations have revealed a number of timber halls and a large sweeping stockade wall. One building contained a Christian shrine and another a Pagan one. This suggests that Gefrin dates from around the time of King Edwin's conversion (AD 627) when the locals were still placing each way bets on the religious stakes. It is said that the missionary, Paulinus, baptized local people in the River Glen later in the same year.

From the bottom of the hill, just before the woods, there are views of Coupland Castle.

A Famous Warrior

The Couplands earned a reputation as a family of mighty warriors. The greatest of them all was Sir John de Coupland who captured Scotland's King David - the son of Robert the Bruce - at the Battle of Neville's Cross in 1346.

According to the chronicler the English attacked a numerically superior force. Although the Archbishop of York was technically the English leader, it was the sword, rather than the mitre that won the day.

Sir John led his own small force of 100 into the thick of the battle. He charged the king and knocked his great battleaxe to the ground. Though unarmed, King David refused to surrender. He lashed out with his gauntleted hand - a blow that gave Sir John a distinctive toothless smile.

Sir John wrestled his man to the ground and took him captive. The English king, Edward III, granted him a pension of £600 a year for his trouble.

The chronicler omits one or two details about the encounter. Other contemporary accounts suggest that the contest was an uneven one. King David's army was weary after the long march to Durham. The King himself was already wounded in the face and leg by the time Sir John tackled him.

King David remained a prisoner for 11 years before Edward III agreed a ransom. He returned to his kingdom and proved to be an effective and respected monarch. There was 'great lamentation' when he died in 1371.

Sir John Coupland was less fortunate. Just a few years later he came second in a sword fight with an English rival. He died from his wounds after lingering in 'unspeakable agony' for three days.

The Rattle Of Chains

Coupland Castle

The castle consists of two square built towers with walls that are seven feet thick. A stair in one tower leads to a 'pepperpot turret' with magnificent views of the 'scenes of blood' enthusiastically described by Sir Walter Scott when he was a visitor. This refers primarily to the battles of Flodden* and Homildon.

An upstairs room features a famous ghost who has, sadly, been inactive since 1925. This spectre was said to be responsible for the dragging of heavy chains and loud echoing footsteps accompanied by the occasional blood chilling wail.

Yeavering Bell

On the opposite side of the road (to the south) there rises the distinctive conical shape of Yeavering Bell.

The hill was once topped by the largest Iron Age fort in Northumbria. Excavations have revealed the foundations of more than 130 oval huts. There is also evidence of paving. Parts of the surrounding stone wall can still be picked out.

The large cairn at the east end is most likely to be the remains of a medieval beacon. For such an important site it is strange that Yeavering Bell has no associations with the supernatural. It is however a favourite haunt of wild mountain goats.

Percy's Revenge

A mile after joining the A697 at Akeld is the site of the Battle of Homildon Hill. A possible battlestone can still be seen in a field just beyond the road junction to Akeld Steads.

This battle - fought on the 14th. September 1402 - was conclusive revenge for the English over the Scots after the ignominy of Otterburn 14 years earlier.

Harry Percy (Hotspur) cut off the retreat of a large Scots raiding force led by Archibald Douglas. The Scots found what appeared to be a good defensive position but were mown down by the English archers. Douglas and the other Scots leaders were captured.

A Grey Lady

The A697 by passes Wooler and the Tankerville Arms is to the left of the road.

This splendid old hostelry features a Grey Lady apparition. There is some doubt as to her identity but a picture in the hostelry has been claimed to reveal a possible candidate.

The Tankerville Arms, Wooler

The Grey Lady had an active haunting record during the second half of the last century. She was seen drifting along corridors and floating through both open and closed doors with equal ease.

It is said that an exorcism around the turn of the century put an end to her activities. Fortunately the other spirits in the hostelry still flow abundantly. The Tankerville Arms has also earned more than a local reputation for good food.

The Trafalgar Connection

The road to Lilburn is a sharp left off the A697 after Haugh Head. Lilburn Grange - immediately on the left - has long been associated with the Collingwood family. A brother of Lord Collingwood, the Admiral who took command of the English fleet after Nelson's death at Trafalgar, created much of the present building and gardens.

The Lilburn Silkie

Tradition has it that a Silkie operates in the wooded areas around the Grange. This is an invisible creature whose presence is announced by a cold draught of wind and a sound like silk rustling in the breeze. Sometimes the chill is accompanied by a mysterious and sudden mist.

Silkies are associated with river sprites and mischievous woodland fairies. If you hear the rustle of silk and feel the icy blast on your face you can be sure that Silkie and her friends are up to no good. People lose their footing on the firmest ground, branches fall with painful consequences for those beneath, and bridges collapse as the unwary walker crosses the stream.

Lilburn Grange

A Spooktacular Castle

Follow the signs to Edlingham and turn right at East Lilburn Farm. This junction is unmarked, but it is just before the farm cottages.

Experienced Ghost Trailers will have noted the signs to Chillingham. It is not featured on this trail, but if you have not enjoyed the special atmosphere of Northumbria's most abundantly haunted castle* the diversion is a must. Chillingham is the most aptly named castle in the world.

The building fell into what looked like terminal disrepair in recent years, but thanks to the enthusiasm of Sir Humphrey Wakefield, the process of restoration is now well advanced. Chillingham Castle is an underrated and unique part of Northumbrian heritage which truly captures the mood of many centuries. Those who take part in the annual Halloween 'Sponsored Spook' will tell you it deserves a full set of marks on the Spectre Scale.

A Haunted Farm

In 1883 the remains of the ancient Lilburn Hill Farm were discovered near here. This building is linked to a notable haunting.

Spooktacular Chillingham

During the 16th. century the local Lord of the Manor was said to have taken a fancy to the daughter of the farmer who worked the land. This was a young lady called Allyson who was famed for her gentle nature, her stunning dark hair, and her shapely figure. The Lord tried a conventional range of strategies to lure this delightful creature into his bed. These were various permutations   of bribery and threats. Allyson refused every advance.

Finally, in desperation, he resorted to simple blackmail. Allyson's family would be thrown out from their living unless she submitted to him. On hearing the news the girl became distraught. The next day she was found hanging from a beam in the barn.

The Lord locked himself away behind the walls of his castle. It was Christmas the following year when he mustered the courage to face them again. He began cautiously by inviting selected tenants to a seasonal feast. He made sure he was heavily surrounded by his henchmen.

It was during the eating of the goose when they noticed that something was wrong. The Lord began to choke and his face took on an unhealthy blackened look. They came to his assistance and someone tried to induce vomiting to help clear poison from his stomach. This tactic merely increased the by now desperate fit of choking.

He began to slide from his chair towards the ground. As they helped him back into the seat he raised an arm and pointed towards the doorway.

" It is she, " he spluttered. " The dark one. "

Looking towards the door they could all see the figure of a dark haired girl. Her shoulders were covered in a blood red cape.

Attention returned to the Lord as he was now successful in collapsing onto the floor. Soon his anguished breathing turned to a death rattle. A stream of blood flowed from one side of his mouth, and a river of black bile flowed from the other.

After two short convulsions he breathed his last.

Eyes turned again to the doorway. The girl had vanished but the cape lay where she had stood. She was never seen again.

A Piece Of Murder

The side road that takes you back to the A697 circles a field known variously as Fleas or Pleas Piece.

In 1811 a journeyman mason was brutally killed in this field. The assassin swapped shoes with his victim and threw the body over a wall.

The corpse was discovered some days later by a shepherd's dog. A tramp was suspected of the murder but nothing was proved.

A Reivers Massacre

Looping back onto the A697 you pass the site of the Battle of Hedgeley Moor.*

The narrow road to Ingram and Brandon is a pleasing approach to one of the most beautiful corners of Northumbria. A small hill to the right reveals medieval fields with their strips and cultivation terraces.

The church opposite the National Park Information Centre dates from the 11th. century. The tower was rebuilt a century ago, but the stones were put back in their original positions. The low, massive shape of the tower suggests it was created with defence in mind.

Park in a small stand of trees past the village and National Park centre.

Ingram was once a significant medieval township. The decline was a gradual one that accelerated during the last two centuries.

In 1587 an army of 500 reivers swept down from Scotland. They attacked Ingram, Prendwick and Ryle. Several men were butchered as they tried to defend their homes. Cattle were taken.

Percy's Leap

A Classic Walk

The ascent of Brough Law is steep but well marked and fairly easy. An hour should be allowed for the 'round trip' walk to the remains of the Iron Age fort.

Cross the road and pick up any of the short tributary paths that lead sharply upwards to the main grassy thoroughfare. If you are using a standard OS map Brough Law is confusingly marked as part of one of three Ewe Hills in the area.

There are the remains of a summer shieling, with the ruins of the perimeter wall marked by hawthorn trees.

The Shepherd's Pie

During the Armstrong raid of 1587 seven of the reivers attacked the shieling but met with spirited resistance from a shepherdess wielding a pitchfork.

One moss trooper was wounded in the neck and another felt the fearsome thrust of the fork in his stomach.

The unmagnificent seven were suitably discouraged and retreated to lick their wounds. An hour later a greater force returned to find that both shepherdess and sheep had escaped to the hills. They looted the simple building but found little apart from a large braxy pie.

The braxy - a local delicacy - was made from diseased meat, often cut from part rotted carcasses. The farmers and shepherds rarely suffered ill effects, but to the unsuspecting reivers the pie was a gastronomic time bomb. Within the hour three of them were suffering. The third took a turn for the worse and died without seeing his home again.

The Teacher's Story

Surprisingly perhaps it is the ghost of the spirited shepherdess that walks Brough Law.

There have been several strange encounters over the years. The most notable was in 1947. Mr. Harold Young, a Tyneside teacher, gave this account:

" I'd been doing some measurements at the fort. I'd planned to draw elevations of how it may have looked in all its former glory. Perhaps I'd been concentrating too much on my work. The mist caught me unawares. "

" I set off down the hill, but turned back when I realised I'd left some instruments. Somehow I managed to lose the path. "

" It had been a sunny August day but it was now close to sunset. I panicked and began to run. Soon I was out of breath and I knew I was lost. I sat on the grass and tried to clear my head. It was going dark now and I was feeling chilled. I cursed myself for leaving my jacket in the car."

" I thought I heard muffled footsteps but I wasn't sure. Then a shape came up from the mist. It was a very tall figure with a shepherd's stick. It came straight to me. I was surprised when I heard a woman's voice. "

" I hardly understood the words. It was a strange throaty dialect. But she knew I was lost. She motioned me to follow her. It seemed no more than a minute or two before we picked up the path by the shieling. I was safe now. The mist had begun to lift and I could see her more clearly. She was about 20 years of age with a face that may have been pretty. It was hard to tell. It had been as long unwashed as her simple clothes. "

" I thanked her and offered her money. I'm not sure she understood".

" Then the odd thing happened. A thick cloud of mist seemed to surround her. But there was nothing round me. We weren't more than ten feet apart. "

" I stepped out towards where she'd stood and the mist retreated before me. I took a step forward. It took a step away. I could almost touch it, but it stayed just beyond the length of my arm. I called out but there was no reply. I knew she'd gone."

" I stopped off at the rectory on the way out of the valley. They were very patient with my questions. There was no one they could think of to match the girl's description. But they told me the story of the shepherdess at the shieling when the Armstrongs came on their famous raid. Yes, I know it was three and a half centuries ago, but I'm sure it was same girl who rescued me."

The Druid Connection

The Brough Law fort you see today is two broken down walls of andesite lava separated by a ditch. In one corner there has been a little model reconstruction.

What has changed less is the magnificent view up the Breamish valley towards Cheviot.

The fort has also been linked with the Druids.

Vortigern - King of the Britons - invited 12 Druids to help him in his campaigns against the Picts and Scots. These Druids were imported from a sacred site in the north of England. There are several possibilities for the location, but Brough Law has perhaps the strongest credentials. Although long past its sell by date as a fortified village, it almost certainly remained an important religious site. The Druids had special status because of their medical skills and wisdom, and they enjoyed the protection of the local population.

Druidism all but died out during the Roman occupation. It was first outlawed by Augustus then violently suppressed by Tiberius. By the middle of the fifth century - 50 years after the collapse of the Roman Empire - the cult had revived enormously.

The Druids have been maligned by history. Mysticism, magic and blood sacrifice are always mentioned. They were part of the cult certainly, but so was the study of natural science, theology, geography and astronomy. They were also a truly democratic society who elected leaders.

Their weakness was a dangerous pacifist tendency. At its worst it encouraged them to place themselves between opposing armies. The new era of Christian kingship that began in the seventh century did not discourage the missionary power of the sword to establish and spread the faith.

The Druids became extinct in Northumbria within ten years of Edwin's conversion.

Queen Mab's Kingdom

After returning to the A697, turn left to Branton, cross the Breamish and pass the pottery on the way to Fawdon. There is ample parking near Croft Cottage but be sure not to obstruct field and farmyard entrances.

Fawdon Hill is Queen Mab's Kingdom - the very heart of Northumbria's world of mystery and enchantment. Queen Mab herself was the undisputed Queen of the Fairies.

Many of the stories come from the 15th. century. The best known is the sad story of the world's worst fairy holocaust.

It is said that a farmer heard a strange kind of music on the hill. Climbing towards the summit he saw the fairies were packed into the area like a Wembley Cup Final crowd.

Eight of the number carried a cup which they brought and offered to him. He panicked, believing that some terrible spell would be cast upon him. He smashed the cup to the ground and wielded his scythe viciously in a wide circle around him.

Estimates of fairy fatalities vary immensely from just a few thousand upwards to a quarter of a million.

From that time onwards Queen Mab ordered her people to live   underground, which perhaps explains why fairies are rarely encountered today.

A Delightful Walk

Take the cart track across the cattle grid. There is a four wheel drive option here, but the walk is easy for all but the most seriously decrepit. Allow around two hours if you take the full route to Ingram and back.

There is a gentle ascent to the cart track crossroads. Turn left to a steeper downhill section towards Ingram. Cutting a corner brings you to the remains of what appears to be a Sandstone trough - actually the base of a ancient cross.

Rituals In Witchcraft

This is the col of East Fawdon Hill, associated with the local covens.

The Fawdon Witches flourished until the middle of the 17th. century. You will still hear stories of 'hell fires' and the bloodthirsty rivalries of the local covens. Fawdon may also have been an excellent place for test-piloting   broomsticks. The thermals make it a favoured spot today for those who enjoy the modern equivalent - hang-gliding.

Crossing the A697 takes you via Beanley to Eglingham. Beanley is most noted for its magnificent stone dovecot - a reminder of the days before we kept emergency food supplies in the freezer.

For the last walk option turn left out of Eglingham towards Chatton and Wooler. Just beyond the edge of the village is a   large farm complex with a bridlepath marked to Ticket Hill.

The Ida Stone

The walk is a short one but sturdy footwear is recommended. Pass the fine stone barns and follow the path down to the ford. The balance and agility of a tightrope walker are required to successfully negotiate the stepping stones - or a pair of wellingtons to negotiate the ford!

The ascent of the first section of the hill is easy. Make for the obvious gate at the top of the field. Below the rocky outcrop is a large fallen stone. This is a strong candidate for the elusive Ida stone, named after the first king of Bernicia.

The story is that this stone was once upright. Ida, who built the mighty fortress at Bebbanburgh (now Bamburgh) was constantly fighting to retain his kingdom. He is sometimes called 'the flamebearer' because of the methods of persuasion he used to secure his position. But scholars still argue about the 'flamebearer' title. It is perhaps more likely to have belonged to his son Theodric.

The Beanley Dovecot

The Eglingham area was popular with the king for hunting. Ida loved the chase and was only truly satisfied when he was thoroughly soaked with blood. On one occasion his quarry escaped. Ida took his revenge on the first inanimate object he encountered - the stone. He dismounted from his horse, walked menacingly towards the sturdy column of rock, and - according to the legend - pushed it over.

Some say this was a carefully stage managed affair. The king had been ill and needed to prove he had recovered his strength. The feat certainly had good publicity value. This was during the third year of his reign - probably AD 549. Ida survived another ten years and died peacefully in his bed.

Scientists offer a less exotic, but perhaps more rational explanation for the random dumping of large chunks of rock such as this. The force that put them there was more powerful than the hand of Ida. In all probability this rock was part of the debris left by a retreating glacier.

The Tankerville Arms at Eglingham is one of the best country pubs in Northumberland. Formerly a coaching inn, it retains the tradition of providing excellent food and ale for the weary traveller.

Phantom Footsteps

The Tankerville Arms is also noted for its ghostly resident. Phantom footsteps have often been heard, and doors seem to open and close themselves. Even when doors have been removed, the sound of them swinging and clicking can still be heard.

One night after the last customer had left, the landlord became so unnerved by the sound of the footsteps that followed him, he ran out into the street.

No explanation has ever been given for this strange ghostly phenomenon...

* Featured in Ghost Trails of Northumbria.

The Tankerville Arms Eglingham

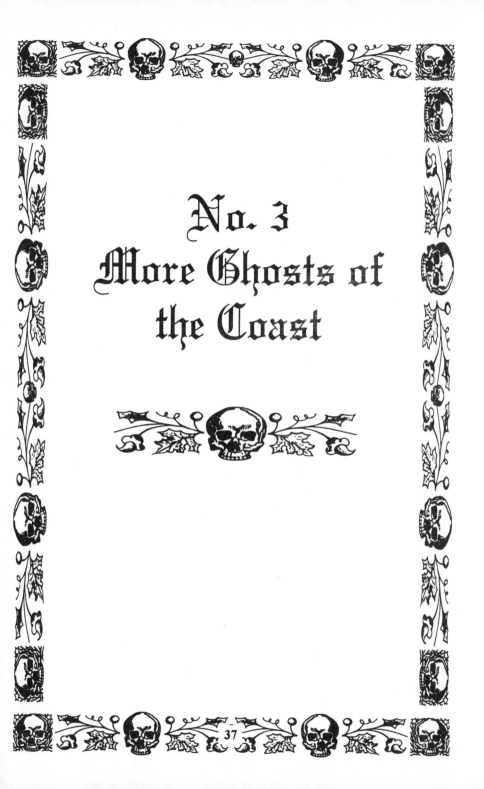

No. 3
More Ghosts of the Coast

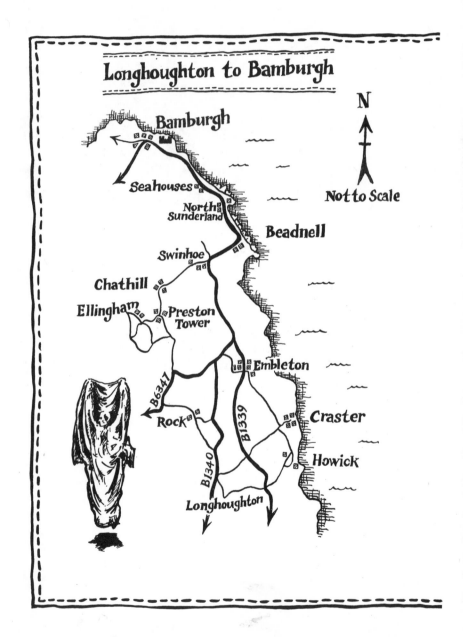

Longhoughton to Bamburgh

N

Not to Scale

Bamburgh

Seahouses

North Sunderland

Beadnell

Swinhoe

Chathill

Ellingham

Preston Tower

B6347

Embleton

Rock

B1339

Craster

B1340

Howick

Longhoughton

This trail alternates between the dramatic Northumbrian coast and some of the lesser known wonders inland.

Longhoughton is a village that has swelled in size in recent years to accommodate forces personnel and civilian workers at RAF Boulmer.

The Smugglers' Hoard

The low square tower of the church and its nave and chancel arch are all Norman. For many years it served as a store for much of the contraband that was brought ashore at Boulmer.

The Bonesetter

Just up from the iron gate by the roadside is the tomb of Isaac Milburn of Longbank. Isaac was a bonesetter of some fame. He used distillations of various herbs to aid the knitting and healing process.

Longhougton Charch

He died in 1886.

A Phantom Fight

On the road to Howick you pass two clumps of woodland by Red Steeds Farm. This was the site of a notable skirmish during the English Civil War.

An escort group, carrying pay for Cromwell's New Model Army, were ambushed by what amounted to a Cavalier vigilante group. The King's men underestimated the resilience of the small escort.

Although they were slain to a man, they made the Cavaliers pay heavily for their prize. After a few minutes of hand-to-hand fighting, around 20 men a dozen of them Cavaliers - lay dead in the road. The King's men loaded the corpses, the wounded, and the heavy chests into a cart. They carried them to a nearby farmhouse.

The chests were forced open with iron bars and found to contain nothing but base metal. The escort had been a well leaked diversion. The real pay patrol had taken a different route.

Strong sunlight can cast strange and fanciful reflections. Travellers have noticed how the branches cast shadows that look like the twisted arms and bodies of men locked in combat. When the wind whistles through the trees that image is particularly strong. The moaning, whistling, and creaking of the timbers adds an eerie soundtrack.

The Downwardly Mobile Nanny

Turn sharp left at Howick Hall. This was once the home of Earl Grey who was Prime Minister at the time of the Reform Bill. The present house was built in 1752 but it was pre-dated by a 15th. century tower. The gardens are open to the public and are well worth a visit. They are considered to be at their very best in May and June.

Howick Hall

From time to time a little old lady has been spotted walking in the garden. She wears the summer costume of a Victorian nanny with a high bonnet.

Observers say she seems to be confused and upset. She mutters to herself and twists.

When you approach, she disappears in an unusual way. Her feet seem to melt into the ground whilst the rest fades into a spectrum gathering the colours of sunlight more and more tightly together before turning into a small orb and vanishing completely.

Records offer no clues to the identity of this strange spirit. There's a theory that a nanny was dismissed from the Hall after accidentally burning her young charge with hot tea. But a second story is more enticing.

A distant relative of the Grey family fell on hard times after the death of her husband. She was taken into the hall and given the job of helping to look after the children.

She loved the garden and also cultivated an affection for the man who looked after it. Whispers about the relationship threatened to bring scandal to the family. The gardener was a married man with grandchildren.

He was quietly redeployed - probably under some duress - to another branch of the Grey family on Tyneside.

The old lady was left with only the comfort of the garden. She developed eccentric habits which included holding long conversations with some of her favourite trees. It was said that she almost became part of the garden.

On one fine September morning she was found cold and dead, but still sitting upright, at the foot of a tree. A fall of golden leaves covered her feet and ankles.

A Long And Violent History

Dunstanburgh Castle can be seen on the skyline on the way to Craster. Standing alone on a rocky outcrop it somehow looks more like an unfinished building site than a ruin. The castle has an illustrious ghost - Margaret of Anjou, the wife of King Henry VI.*

This virtually impregnable fortress was built by Thomas, Earl of Lancaster in 1313.

Harbinger Of Death?

Craster Tower is on the right just before the archway.

It is a Georgian farmhouse built around an early 15th. century tower made from the local whinstone. It is not open to the public.

Dunstanburgh Castle

The Crasters first inhabited this spot in Saxon times. The family was one of the few that were allowed to retain their possessions after the Conquest. This represents more than 900 years of occupation by the same family.

The raven insignia, part of the Craster coat of arms, has sometimes mistakenly been given sinister significance. Earlier spellings of the name - Craucester or Crewster - are better clues to the origin. The raven is a pun on the family name. This is much the same as the interpretation of scaling ladder in the Grey crest. It comes from the old French word - gre - which means a flight of steps.

The Mysterious Men In Black

There is pocket of land near Craster Tower where it is said no plants will grow. This was once where a local fishing family lived.

According to the legend the fisherman, Jacob, was busy mending nets one day when a group of unusual visitors arrived. There were around two dozen men all dressed in black. They have been variously described as monks or druids.

They asked for food and water and Jacob provided what he could. He was poorly repaid for his generosity. One of the men drew a knife and plunged it deep into Jacob's back.

It was at this moment that the fisherman's wife, Ruth, entered the cottage with their baby daughter. Her eyes took in the dreadful scene at once and she tried to escape. One of the men near the door made a grab for her and the child. She wrestled herself free of his grasp but fell near the fireplace.

As they closed in around her she took a burning wand of wood from the fire and waved it in their faces. The mob parted like the sea for Moses. She struggled back to the doorway using one arm to wave the wand and the other to support her baby.

When she was safely into the light she turned and threw the burning stick back towards the doorway. Her aim was poor. The thatch was alight almost immediately.

She did not stay to watch, but began to run towards the harbour.

The men in black pushed and jostled with each other in a bid to escape the blazing cottage. Those who first escaped from the flames set off in pursuit of the woman and child.

Suddenly the sound of laughing and singing rang through the trees. A group of fishermen, who had enjoyed a successful day at their work, were on their way home. Their voices were silenced as they approached the clearing where the cottage was ablaze. Then they saw Ruth and the men who pursued her.

The men leapt from their carts and seized whatever primitive weapons they could. A few minutes later all but one of the men in black lay dead. The last ran back towards the cottage and stood by the doorway. The fishermen followed and surrounded him with their bloodstained axes and pitchforks.

The fishermen heard the man shout a curse, but the words were partly drowned out by the cracking and crashing of the timbers. For a moment the man in the doorway hesitated. All he had left was the choice of his fate.

He turned and walked through the doorway into the inferno.

The First Kipper

They found his body later amongst the burnt remains of the cottage. It is said that the corpse was in a curious condition. It was not charred or burned beyond recognition but preserved and cooked by the smoke.

Did this event have far reaching consequences?

Today's visitors to Craster delight in the delicate flavour of the world's finest kippers, and an increasing variety of other smoked fish. The tradition of local smokehouses can be traced back for centuries - perhaps to the day when mysterious men in black came to a fisherman's door asking for food and water...

The Phantom Fishing Boat

Park at Craster's Tourist Information Centre and enjoy the short walk down to the harbour.

Although the region's fishing industry has declined in recent years Craster survives as a working harbour. Some of the fishermen still put to sea in the small boats - or cobles - based on a superbly seaworthy design that has stood the test of centuries.

The world's first lifeboat was a specially adapted coble that was patented by a London coachbuilder in 1785 and put into full service at Bamburgh the following year. But for years before that time daring rescues at sea were carried out by fishermen in their own boats.

Craster Harbour

A bizarre tale is set in that pre-lifeboat era - probably during the early part of the 18th. century. It was a time, very much like today, when the fisherman's livelihood was precarious.

On a day in early autumn part of the fleet were fishing closely together in one area when a sudden storm blew up. One of the boats was hit by a monster wave and capsized. The skippers of two other boats, who were close enough to see what had happened, went to the rescue.

They found the men clinging to the upturned hull of their stricken craft and threw them a line. As soon as the last man was safely rescued the overturned boat was hit by another large wave. For a moment the small vessel seemed to half right herself before turning bottom up again and drifting away with the force of the gale.

The storm was blowing heavily from the west and it took several hours of great effort to battle to the safe haven of the harbour. As they approached, both the rescuers and rescued were close to the end of their strength.

But as they entered the small harbour they noticed something familiar. Already tied up was the same coble that had drifted away from them on the open sea. More improbably - according to the story - the small craft was undamaged and still contained her nets and catch.

Not only had the men been rescued, but through some strange intervention, their precious livelihood had also been preserved.

The Rocky Road

The route to Rock follows a maze of small lanes. The use of a large scale map is recommended because signposting is confusing and inadequate.

Leave the village and pass Craster Tower before crossing straight over at the next junction. Then turn right onto the B1339, right again at crossroads towards Rennington, and right yet again towards Christon Bank. After a mile you turn left towards Rock. There is a final right turn before the village. Last of all, turn left at the phone box and park by the church and Post Office.

An Unexpected Delight

The village is a small gem. Visitors are constantly surprised that such a place exists in what is essentially a flat agricultural wilderness.

Much of what you see today has been created through the efforts of a man who knew a great deal about wilderness.

There is a churchyard inscription to Charles Bosanquet who was buried here in 1850. It states that ' as Governor of the Canada Land Company he was instrumental in bringing into cultivation large tracts of land in Canada West.'

It was Charles who completed the work of dividing a feudal estate into farms. He also restored the church, rebuilt much of the village, and repaired and added to the hall which had been destroyed by fire and allowed to fall into ruin.

The church is worth a visit. The west doorway is a well weathered Norman original and the chancel arch also features the zigzag mouldings that first became fashionable in the 11th. century.

A Turnip For The Book

Blue markers indicate a popular local walk that skirts the grounds of the hall.

There is also a small part of Northumbrian history in many of the fields. Early in the 18th. century a famous gardener, Andrew Willy, pioneered the growing of turnips for cattle feed.

Sweet Rock Hall

This fine ivy covered building, which dates from the 15th. century, was until recently a youth hostel. It is now a successful school.

In its early days the battlemented tower was garrisoned by soldiers who served against the Scots. In these days of Euro-partnership it is worth noting that Sir Julian Romero's mercenaries were mainly Germans, Italians and Spaniards.

The Ghostly Cavalier

In Norman times the manor was held by the De Rock family under the barony of Alnwick. Most recently it has been associated with the Proctor and Bosanquet families. But the most famous owner of all was John Selkeld who served Charles I with 'a constant, dangerous and expensive loyalty as volunteer captain and colonel of horse.'

There was fierce rivalry between Colonel Selkeld and the master of Capheaton Hall - John Swinbourne. The grudge each man had for the other has never been fully understood. It may have been political, or based on envy. There are rumours too that there was rivalry over a certain raven haired lady.

John Selkeld stabbed John Swinbourne through the heart as they argued in front of the gates of Meldon. There were more than a dozen witnesses. An inquest returned a verdict of wilful murder and the colonel must have expected the worst. Surprisingly he escaped without penalty. He had proved himself just too valuable to the royalist cause. At times of national crisis, justice is overtaken by expediency.

John Selkeld lived for another 32 years. It is said that people heard noises from inside his coffin just before he was buried.

Rock Hall

Since that time a ghostly cavalier has been a major feature at Rock Hall. He walks the corridors in a distinctive cockaded wide brimmed hat. He whispers outside rooms - particularly on the upper floors. He is blamed for any amount of paranormal activity including the moving of objects from one place to another. When in 1752 the Hall burnt down local people had few doubts as to who was responsible...

A Grey Lady

Behind the hall is the Lady's Well. From time to time a most chilling apparition has been seen in this vicinity. It is Rock Hall's famous Grey Lady.

The Cyclist's Story

The following incident took place on August 15th. 1969. The story is narrated by Janet Frost of Berwick.

" I'd been doing a bicycle tour of the coast with some friends. We'd decided to stay at the Youth Hostel. "

" I woke up in the middle of the night feeling very hot. I tried to get back to sleep but it was impossible. So I pulled on my jeans and sweater and went downstairs. I thought I'd raid the fridge for something cold to drink."

" When I got downstairs I noticed the main door was open. I tried to push it closed but the lock was jammed. Outside the moonlight was really bright. I was bare footed but I stepped outside to have a better look. "

" It was really beautiful. The trees were like giant silhouettes in front of the old church tower. There were some rabbits feeding on the grass. Best of all, it was really cool. I felt the dew between my toes. I don't know why, but I suddenly wanted to go for a walk around. "

" I was round the back of the hall near the Lady's Well when I had the feeling that someone was following me. I looked around. There was nobody there. But then suddenly I saw her. She was coming straight across the grass. She was a small lady in a cloak that skimmed the ground. I remember thinking that the cloak seemed to be too large and too heavy for her. "

" I thought she was coming to tell me off. No, I don't know why. Maybe it was the way she was moving. She was in such a hurry. But then it all changed. "

" She went straight past me as if I wasn't there. I followed her with my eyes. She was moving even faster now. It was really funny. It wasn't like walking at all. It was more like skating on ice. "

" She was going so fast that when she reached the wall of the building I was sure she'd crash into it. I tried to shout but I couldn't make a sound. The noise was strangled in my throat. "

" She went straight through that wall without a sound. It was unreal - just like a cartoon come to life. I stared at the spot where she'd vanished. I couldn't believe what I'd seen."

" Then I started to shake. I remember my teeth were rattling together. They've never done that before or since. I couldn't move at first. It was like being frozen to the ground. But then I was walking, but I still couldn't take my eyes away from that wall. "

" When I reached the corner I started to run. I could hear my heart beating faster and faster. I thought it was going to burst. But I didn't stop running until I reached the front door. I rushed to grab the handle. I pulled as hard as I could. It was no use. The door was locked. "

" I rang the bell. Nothing seemed to happen. I started to feel faint and sick. Suddenly the door opened and the warden was standing there in his pajamas. He'd one of those heavy rubber torches in his hand. "

I tried to tell him about what had happened but I don't think he believed a word. He took me to the kitchen and calmed me down. But I could tell he wasn't pleased about being woken up. He thought I'd slipped out of a window to meet a boyfriend or something. The door had been locked since ten o'clock... "

Explaining The Wall

Janet Frost's encounter with the Grey Lady raises two interesting questions. Just who is the mysterious Grey Lady and why does she appear to float through a wall?

Local tradition suggests that in life the Grey Lady was Arabella Lawson, wife of Henry Lawson, the brother of an Elizabethan owner of the hall.

The story is that Arabella was staying with a relative at South Charlton when she had a premonition that all was not right at the hall. So strong was the feeling that she rose from her bed in the middle of the night and set out to walk the few miles between the villages.

When the hall came into view she increased her pace. Finally she was running. Just as she reached the doorway a priest was stepping out into the night air. Her fears proved to be fully justified. The priest had just given the last rites to her husband. The unfortunate Henry had fallen from his horse some hours earlier and the sharp spines of the furze had torn deep into his neck and severed an artery.

Arabella was just in time to be at her husband's side as he breathed his last.

Could it be that on August 15th. each year - the anniversary of the accident - the shade of Arabella Lawson walks the same weary way from South Charlton to Rock Hall?

The wall is possibly easier to explain. At the time of the accident the hall was still essentially a medieval fortress comprising of an large oblong tower with two smaller towers linked to it. The walls which the ghost floats through so effortlessly were not constructed until the 17th. century.

The Haunted Hiker

A local man tells another strange story of the days when the hall was a hostel.

It seems that a young hiker woke one morning to find a strange figure sitting at the end of his bed. It was another hiker.

But as the clouds of sleep evaporated the young man realised there was something strange about his visitor. His clothes, from his shirt to his boots, seemed to have been picked out of a museum.

The young man reached down beside the bed and took hold of his own boot. He pulled it upwards, took aim, and threw it. The boot seemed to pass right through the middle of the phantom who promptly disappeared.

Preston Tower

The route to Preston Tower is via Christon Bank, turning left at the Blink Bonney before taking the road to Seahouses.

This fortress is mentioned as early as 1415. The first known owner was Robert Harbottle. It is said that building began in 1392.

What remains is essentially half of the old fortress but it is nevertheless well worth a visit. The original was an oblong building with turrets at the four corners. A scale model shows what it looked like six centuries ago.

Much of the restoration took place during the 1860's. Mason's marks can be clearly picked out on the stonework. The

Preston Tower

present owners have made great efforts to capture the mood of days long gone by. There is a guardroom and prison on the ground floor. On the first is a bedroom and living room furnished in the manner of the late 14th. and or early 15th. century.

The tower also features an ear shattering clock that was installed in 1864.

A Phantom Hound

At one side of the tower there are traces of cottages that were   removed around the time of the Restoration.

It is here that the Preston Hound has been seen. It's a creature that makes a pit bull terrier seem as intimidating as a pipe and slippers spaniel.

The beast is said to be as tall as a pony. He is heavy set with mighty shoulders and the neck of an ox. His coat is shiny black and his fangs are gleaming white. His eyes shine with a wild glow of rage.

It is said that such a creature was once employed to discourage unwelcome visitors. No doubt he was successful is his vocation.

But in the end he became uncontrollable even to his keepers. They kept him hungry for as long as they dared then fed him meat that had been soaked in poison.

As the agony racked his body the beast broke from his chains and set upon those who had brought him his death. Their bodies were so savagely mutilated it was no longer possible to say which limb had been attached to which person. The arms and legs had been severed in the way that a chainsaw runs through a pile of logs. The faces were unrecognisable. The torsos had been torn and shredded into untidy heaps of raw flesh and bloodstained cloth.

But in death the hound remained loyal to his masters. It is said that he will only appear if those at the tower or the farm are threatened by intruders. This excellent arrangement has been described as a Neighbourhood Watchdog Scheme.

A Divided Village

Nearby Ellingham is a village divided east and west.

The church can be located by following a narrow dead end track. From the churchyard there are fine views over the sea and to Preston Tower. Distinctive stones line the path from the gate to the church door. They look like medieval prototype carvings of space rockets.

The church itself contains a fine window in the north transept that shows the stages of the creation. The most striking panels represent the beasts, the birds, the fish and the flowers.

Ellingham Hall features a pair of prancing lions on the gatepost. The small Roman Catholic chapel attached to the house was begun around 1600.

The Packhorse Inn is a country pub with real character. As the name implies this was once a shoeing and stabling stop as well as a coach staging post. Ellingham is close to the A1 - the ancient and modern route to Berwick and Scotland.

At one time a member of the Haggerston family - supporters of the Stuart cause - bribed a driver to overturn his coach. The main passenger was the notorious 'Butcher' Cumberland. The Haggerstons had been ordered to arrange transport and protection for the Duke between Belford and Berwick - a task they must have welcomed as much as a dose of dysentery.

Ellingham Church

A Longrunning Race

Imagine the scene. The first light of day casts a pale amber glow on the village's main street. From behind the Packhorse Inn you hear the echo of a loud curse. Next there is the sound of flying hooves and a sturdy bay mare canters into the street. She shakes her head and whinnies, prances on her heels for a moment, then makes off westward at a purposeful gallop.

A small red faced man rounds the corner from the stables. He sees the mare in full flight, throws his hat to the ground, and begins to give chase.

This scene in itself is more entertaining than unusual. What makes it interesting to the ghost-trailer is the way it was witnessed several times during

Pack Horse Inn, Ellingham

the second half of the 19th. century. Then, in the years just before the First World War, it became an almost routine event.

There are eye-witness accounts from 1904, 1911, and 1913. All are similar in detail. One of them refers - perhaps significantly - to 'oftimes before.' No explanation of the phenomena is ever offered and the identity of neither of the leading characters in the spooky scenario are revealed. The last account of this drama - at least as played out for public benefit - comes from 1921. The details again are much the same but with one important difference. The man is now much sharper in the pursuit of the steed. At one point be makes a grab for the bridle and misses by no more than a whisker.

Accounts of 'ghost chases' are not rare. Perhaps the most famous is that of the masked executioner chasing a headless victim around Tower Green. As sightings develop the pursuer inevitably gets closer and closer to the pursued. It is assumed that he finally catches is quarry and the manifestation is then filed away under 'Old Haunts'.

Judging by the progress of the Ellingham groom this scene may have played to its last audience in the 1920's. It would have seemed unexceptional to anyone unless they knew that the show had run for longer than The Mousetrap. Horse escapes from stable. Man catches horse. End of story.

A local observation is that the ghostly groom put in extra training between 'performances'. It was this peak of preparedness and fitness that finally helped him to get a result...

There may be a hidden deeper message there somewhere. It is left to the reader to decide if that is worth considering.

A Fairy Dance

Tradition has it that there was once a fairy ring at Chathill. Sadly there is no evidence of either fairy or ring today.

At one time an unusual dance would take place at night. Nine children would dance nine times round the ring. This apparently brought good fortune.

The station is as neglected as a wild west ghost town in the old B movies. There's no tumbleweed here but there are rattles and creaks as these sad buildings try to hold out against the wind for just a little bit longer.

A Celebrated Case

The B1340 leads to North Sunderland. There is little enough activity here even on a fine summer day. But on such a day in September 1844 five hundred local people marched down the street carrying an effigy on poles. Two days later they fired and looted a property belonging to a local doctor.

The reason for this unrest can be traced back to February of the previous year. It was in that month that a certain Dr Belaney married a local heiress - Rachel Skelly.

The worthy doctor immediately took his mother-in-law's business affairs in hand. Two months later she died from what Belaney described as an acute bilious fever.

Rachel inherited the property and business, and in May made a will in favour of her husband.

The following spring Belaney decided to take his pregnant wife to London. They took up lodgings there on 4th. June. The following day he brought prussic acid and other drugs from a pharmacy. On June the 8th. Rachel became seriously ill. The landlady was unhappy with Belaney's diagnosis of heart disease and insisted on a second opinion. A Doctor Garrett arrived to witness Rachel's last moments. He accepted Belaney's diagnosis but insisted on a post mortem.

A pint of prussic acid was taken from Rachel Belaney's stomach.

The trial was a confused affair. Belaney insisted that the acid had been purchased for his own heart condition and that his wife had swallowed it thinking it was water. Much of the evidence was circumstantial and related to circumstances surrounding the death of Mrs Skelly and letters that Belaney had written to his steward. In essence Belaney's defence was that he was careless, even neglectful, but he was certainly no murderer.

The jury believed him. He was free to return to North Sunderland in early September as a man of considerable substance.

But local people were less sympathetic than the London jury. In the riots that followed, Belaney was forced to defend himself by firing a pistol into the crowd outside his house.

He escaped to Alnwick but was recognised by regulars at the Willow Tree Inn. They blackmailed him for beer money.

The special sessions that followed the North Sunderland riots followed a similar pattern to the earlier trial. Many accusations were made against individual ringleaders but there were no convictions.

Belaney returned to North Sunderland. He was last seen around the end of October, then suddenly he disappeared.

He has not been seen or heard of since...

All Aboard For The Islands

Seahouses harbour is a different world to the miniature resort behind it.

It is one of the few really active small ports left in the region, though even here an increasing number of former fishermen are earning a living by offering their boats to the rod and line men, and by running pleasure trips for the tourists.

Seahouses is the staging post for the Farne Islands. Here the colonies of grey seals, cormorants and puffins delight the visitors. There is also the famous Longstone Light, now unmanned, associated with Bamburgh heroine Grace Darling.*

On a fine, still day when the sea is blue, a trip to the islands is a delight. But the North Sea cannot be tamed. The countless wrecks around these shores are a measure of the daily peril faced by the mariners. There are days when only the brave or foolhardy will leave the protective walls of the harbour. It is perhaps a surprise then that the most famous local ghost is a woman.

The Sad Tale Of A Working Girl

Seahouse Harbour

Mary Elizabeth Dodd was not a local girl, but a First World War evacuee from Newcastle.

She came to stay with distant relatives who were happy to have an extra pair of hands around the house as so many of the menfolk were away from home. The family, like many in Seahouses today, relied on both the sea and the wallets of visitors to make a living.

Mary came to love Seahouses. Years later she said that the natives were as wild and unpredictable as the sea itself. But perhaps this tells us more about Mary than the local people. She liked to live her life close to the edge of the precipice.

The Farne Islands were the fantasy world of her innocence. When she could she went out with the fishermen and wondered at the weather beaten rock stacks and their colonies of birds.

But her new family were disappointed in her. She proved to be clumsy when it came to mending nets and lobster pots. She was accident prone in the kitchen. She was a real menace with a needle in her hand.

The family desperately tried to find something she was good at. Mary was at least keen and presentable when it came to waiting at table. But in the end it was the girl herself who found the real answer.

It began when the family boarded a visitor from Scotland. He was a lonely middle aged man who was delighted by the attention paid to him by the flame haired girl. He couldn't help noticing that although she was not long past her 14th. birthday, she already had the ample physical attributes of a mature woman.

It was a cold night no doubt, and Mary was never less than obliging. In the morning she was delighted to find that two shiny threepences had been left in her slipper. She may have been clumsy of hand, but she was quick enough in the head. In that moment a career was born.

The family must have been encouraged by the way the visitor trade picked up. But did it not seem just a little strange that most of the guests were single men at a time when the species was something of a rarity?

After the war Mary stayed on in Seahouses. Some people must have raised their eyebrows when they heard she had saved enough money to open a guest house of her own. But things went well for her. Within a year she recruited two more girls to help her run the establishment.

This gave Mary more time to enjoy the open air. She was often seen on the sea front staring out towards the islands. She also spent many happy hours walking along the harbour walls and chatting to the fishermen.

But then things began to go wrong. In part this was because Mary Dodd was a woman of fashion, but the corseted and tight bound 'boyish' style of the period was ill suited to her generous proportions. And Seahouses was the wrong place to flaunt the fashion. It drew attention to her. It set tongues wagging.

It is likely that Mary's courageous attempts at style and her various entrepreneurial skills were applauded by local men in private. In public however they were finally forced to denounce her. The unofficial, but powerful, union of fishermen's wives wanted to be rid of Mary Elizabeth Dodd.

She knew it was time to move on. The prospect made her miserable but she faced it with courage. The property was sold and Mary left the village forever.

That would have been the end of the story but for a bizarre coincidence. Five years later Mary was recognised by a Seahouses man in a Newcastle suburb. He had just shared a few pints with city friends when he spotted an affluent but ampler Mary about to climb into a Rolls Royce.

He was overcome with joy at seeing an old friend, particularly one who had clearly furthered her career. He rushed up to her and gave her a beery kiss and a big hug.

From the loud comments that followed it was clear they had once been well acquainted. The fisherman assumed that the distinguished looking man already seated in the car was an up market client.

Unfortunately, this was not the case. The man was a solicitor of some substance and a Justice of the Peace. More importantly, he happened to be Mary's husband.

This moment of indiscretion led to an unhappy chain of events. Mary Dodd was at one moment respectable, and the next cast out and friendless.

Time and the good life had also taken its toll of her. She had lost not only her figure but also the best of her health.

It's said she returned to work - mainly on Newcastle's quayside. Less than a year later a clergyman found her huddled and wheezing in an alleyway. She was wearing little more than what had once been an expensive fur coat.

Mary was taken to hospital. She died of pneumonia less than a week later.

A Lonely Vigil

From time to time the figure of a woman is seen on the green sward above the beach. She wears a short skirt, a clinging top, and a wide brimmed hat - very much the uniform of the 'Flapper' era.

This lonely figure stands stock still and stares out towards to islands. It is always in the same place and is generally seen on the pleasanter of summer days.

The odd thing about the figure is that it seems to vanish almost as soon as it is seen. Visitors have remarked on it. Many of the locals have little idea what it may mean. Is this a ghost or a mirage?

By the early 1990's there were just a few of the very oldest male inhabitants who knew the answer. Only one was prepared to tell the whole story. Others perhaps suffered from diplomatic amnesia. They'd tell you but little, but then again they always spoke with a smile on their lips...

A Magnificent Monument

There is no castle in Britain that captures the imagination better than Bamburgh. It is partly to do with scale and partly with setting.

The history of Bamburgh Castle* is a distinguished and turbulent one. The monument is now in the safe keeping of the Armstrong family.

Northumbrian Heroines

Both the small Grace Darling* museum and the castle are worth visiting. Grace, foremost amongst English heroines, is buried in St. Aidan's churchyard. The crypt houses the tomb of the equally remarkable Dorothy Forster.

The Famous Forsters

The Forster family are forever associated with Bamburgh. Four of their graves are found in the tiny crypt. It is a chilling place, once lost for almost a century. Old bones and older gravestones are scattered around the walls.

Here you feel uncomfortably close to the past. When the crypt was 'rediscovered' by Archdeacon Thorpe in 1847 it must have been a pitiful sight. There were five coffins on a stone platform containing the bodies of important members of the Forster family. The coffins were in various stages of decay. One of them had fallen to pieces. It contained the remains of Dorothy Forster. The ribbon which had tied the jaw to the rest of the skull was lying on the floor.

Even today, The slabs that cover the tombs of Dorothy and her brother Tom Forster are rarely seen by visitors. This makes them even more poignant reminders of one of the most famous stories in Northumbrian history.

A Celebrated Escape

Tom Forster found himself as the rather unlikely choice as General of the English forces who rose in support of the Stuart cause in 1715. They were soundly defeated at Preston and Tom was imprisoned in Newgate.

Nobody knows how Dorothy engineered his escape. It is said she left Bamburgh in the company of a local blacksmith and made the three week journey to London. They got hold of a key, and possibly with the help of bribery and disguise, they managed to smuggle Tom out of the prison.

Sand And Sawdust

When the crypt was opened in the last century it's said that one of the coffins contained nothing but sand and sawdust. Had this been part of the plot? A mock funeral for Tom perhaps? It is known he escaped to France and died abroad. His body was returned and buried in Bamburgh in 1738.

It seems ironic that Northumberland's two greatest heroines should be buried less than a hundred yards from each other. The visitors who flock to Bamburgh each year have a church window, two memorials, and a museum to remind them of Grace Darling. Dorothy Forster, whose courage at least matched that of amazing Grace, is to most tourists anonymous and unknown.

Death In The Afternoon

Another famous Forster grave belongs to Ferdinando who died in an infamous duel.

During the summer of 1701 he was drinking with friends at Newcastle's Black Horse Tavern. John Fenwick of Rock, an enemy of Ferdinando's, came into the tavern and began singing a song which Ferdinando took as an insult.

An argument began and Ferdinando challenged John Fenwick to a duel. They stepped into the street but Ferdinando, who was certainly the worse for drink, fell before he could draw his sword. John Fenwick settled the argument by running his sword through his enemy before his balance was recovered.

There was an outcry from the Forsters for justice. A month later Fenwick was hung at the same spot. Ferdinando's armour, which we assume he wasn't wearing on that fateful August afternoon, is still preserved in the church.

Marry Young For A Long Life

A group of gravestones in the churchyard evoke memories of another noted local family, the Younghusbands. One of their number - Thomas - made his own mark in local folklore. The evidence of the tombstone says it all. The inscription reads : ' Thomas Younghusband. Born 1669. Died 1771'. In 18th. century Northumberland, average life expectancy was 47 years.

Another gravestone is marked with a familiar carving. It is sometimes called the pirate's grave, but the skull and crossbones is usually interpreted as a symbol of mortality.

Treasures Of History

The greatest treasures of history are to be found in the church building itself.

There is the first Grace Darling memorial, brought into the building to prevent further erosion a century ago. The canopied replacement in the churchyard now looks rather more a victim of the weather.

St. Aidan's shrine, close to the spot where he died, is placed before a leper's stoop. It is a small window where those afflicted with the disease queued up to receive alms, food and Holy Communion. Then there is the superb crusader's effigy. As effigies were usually life size you look down at the shape of a man who would have been a giant by the standards of the 12th. century.

Tradition has it that this is Sir Lancelot. The Arthurian legend has often been linked to Bamburgh. One problem with this Sir Lancelot is the little matter of the six centuries that divide the effigy from the Romano/British roots of the legend.

Perhaps the greatest treasure of all is St. Aidan's beam. Although it has survived two great fires and generations of relic hunters, it is now placed some 30 feet above the ground for its best protection.

An American tourist once asked a church guide if it was true that St.Aidan was lying close to the beam during his final hours. He was told that this was the tradition. The American's eyes stared at the beam. 'So just how did he get up there? ' he asked.

The Plunderers

Bamburgh was once associated with the plundering of wrecks. This tradition goes back at least to 1492 when the St. Salvador, on route from Flanders, came to grief on nearby rocks. She was carrying a cargo of rich merchandise.

Bamburgh Castle

There was extra profit to be made from taking a valuable hostage. The Abbot of St. Columbane, a passenger on the ill-fated ship, was ransomed for 80.

The Eerie Song Of The Sea

On the rocks below Bamburgh's lighthouse a strange melodious voice can sometimes be heard.

Some say it is the whistling of the wind or the roar of the tide. Others claim it is more than that.

The sound has been described as similar to the chant of plainsong. It is always a single voice. It fades and swells then fades again. The words are intoned in a strange tongue. Some who have heard it claim it is Latin. Others say it is a language they have never heard before.

This plaintive song is not associated with any known incident or phenomenon. The reader is left to ponder the mystery.

* Featured in Ghost Trails of Northumbria

No. 4
Around
Coquetdale

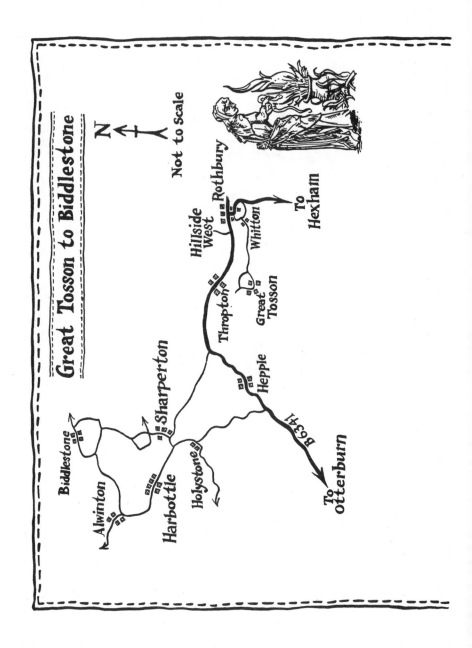

Great Tosson to Biddlestone

N

Not to Scale

Coquetdale is one of the loveliest valleys in England. It is hard to think of anywhere better to enjoy the sense of being close to the past.

This trail begins at Great Tosson, two miles south west of Rothbury. The 'great' suggests a habitation of some size. But in the wilds of Northumberland size is a relative thing. Nevertheless 'great' serves as a comparison with the late prehistoric encampment - Tosson Burgh - on the ridge above, and Tosson Mill - a tiny hamlet close to the riverside below.

A Noble Ruin

The present condition of Great Tosson Tower - 'a ragged shell of a pele with the highest fragments of walls about 30 feet high' - is due to centuries of decay. This was once ' part of Lord Ogle's inheritance'. A survey carried out during the reign of Henry VIII reveals that the tower was already badly neglected.

Tosson Tower

Most of the facing stones have been taken for local building. What you see today is mainly the rubble core of walls. These were made from small rocks taken from the river and cemented together with hot lime. It's a building method that obviously worked. What's left of the tower seems likely to survive even the Northumbrian climate for several centuries to come.

Local Defences

The pele was part of the chain of castles and towers in the Coquet Valley. When Robert Bruce destroyed Hepple Tower (c. AD 1310) the De Hepple family moved their 'court' to Tosson. For a few years it became a place of some importance. Records tell us that each night two men kept watch from the high walls for any sign of Scots hostility. A rider was also permanently employed - ready to be 'despatched with haste' - to warn others of an attack.   Other contingency plans included the 'constant readiness to light the great beacon' on Simonside.

Mistaken Identity

In was during this period, in 1337, that a case of mistaken identity had tragic consequences.

A patrol of soldiers from the tower had been set upon by members of the Armstrong 'clan' near Elsdon. In a brief skirmish one of the soldiers was wounded and was carried to a dwelling near Duns Farm.

The wound proved not to be serious, but the patrol leader decided it was wiser to rest overnight rather than risk an attack in the dark when they were carrying a casualty.

The sentries at Tosson had long expected the return of the patrol and became nervous when darkness fell. One of them spotted a line of torches approaching from below and the remaining men-at-arms were called to the walls in readiness. The   number of torches suggested a large body of men. No   visitors were expected so the small garrison had their welcome ready when   the column came within range. They fired off as many arrows as they could and were rewarded by several screams from below.

The column retreated, then a single rider approached carrying a banner. This was a signal for truce. The man was met outside the walls by the garrison commander.

The banner proved to be that of King Edward himself. The soldiers were part of a large detachment of mercenaries who had been sent to shore up the defences of the March.

Two of the men had wounds and a third was found dead in the bed of the stream that flowed by the walls of the tower. A healthy set of teeth might perhaps have saved him but these had long since rotted to stumps.

The arrow had passed without resistance between his lips and was lodged in the back of his throat.

A Haunted Stream?

For many years after the incident the stream was said to be unlucky, even haunted.

But there is confusion here. The stories of a hideously stunted figure floundering and falling on the stones bear no obvious comparison to the tragic accident. It is more likely to be the famous Simonside Deugar on route to his lair for a cannibal supper.*

The Miller's Daughter

The tale of Katherine the miller's daughter originates from the turn of the 15th. century.

Katherine, who was born at Tosson Mill, grew up to be a famous beauty. Although short of stature, she was 'bold as a vixen' and could charm any man with a smile. It is said that before she reached puberty she had caused a jealous fight between the young men of Whitton and Rothbury.

But Katherine was determined to make her beauty work for her at a higher level. Rather like the groupies of modern times she began her 'apprenticeship' with the local garrison. Her reputation spread and she soon found favour with William Tailbois, the soldier son of a noted local family.

This was the inspiration she needed. From Tailbois it was not too great a step to the object of her ambitions - Harry Percy, known as Hotspur.

There have been whispers down the centuries that Hotspur earned his nickname for reasons other than impulsive acts of valour. Whether this was true or not, he obviously had what it takes to encourage fidelity. After Katie met Harry she never looked at another man.

Unhappily the great man soon tired of the miller's daughter. These were troubled times, and whilst Hotspur had time for affairs, he also had to consider the affairs of state. Other women and other minor matters - such as planning the next campaign - were constant distractions for him.

Nevertheless, he recognised that Kate had qualities that would be wasted on common men. He therefore offered to pass Katherine on to his uncle, Thomas, Earl of Worcester.

Katherine didn't think much of this arrangement, which was apparently rather like swapping D'Artagnan for Quasimodo.

" Better than he, " she told Hotspur, " would be to go to a nunnery." Hotspur made the arrangements and Katherine entered the sisterhood at York.

One conclusion of the story has Katherine taking her own life after hearing of Hotspur's death at Shrewsbury. Another version has her returning to Coquetdale, marrying, and spending the rest of her days as a respected member of the community.

A Spectral Song

Below the site of the mill is a flat expanse of land running down to the riverside.

From time to time an unusual spectre has been seen walking on the mill side of the river. It is the figure of a woman, dressed in the habit of a nun, singing a ballad that mourns the loss of a lover.

Whilst this is singularly rare in itself, it is also an unusual apparition in other ways. No observer has ever seen the features of a face which is usually turned away. The tune that is sung is always recognised by those who hear it, but strangely they can never put a name to it or even sing a few notes from memory.

The Photographer's Story

Daniel Wilson, a photographer from Saltburn, witnessed this phenomenon as recently as 1989. He describes what happened like this :

" It's not like seeing a ghost. The woman looks solid and normal. But who expects to meet a nun walking a muddy path and singing to herself? It was the strangest thing that's ever happened to me."

" MacEnroe, my border terrier, was with me. He chased towards her down the path. Then he stopped, barked, and rushed back. Mac was shaking. He's never been scared of anything - not even thunder. He stayed tucked in close behind my heels until we'd passed her."

" I wanted to say something - anything - about the song. It was weird, just a few notes repeated over and over again. It was like icy fingers down your spine. It was the saddest thing I've ever heard. The words seemed to float in the air. "

" As I got close I looked at her face. It was a real shock. That face was like a blank page - nothing. But I only saw it for a second. She quickly turned away from me. I walked past and looked round. I couldn't help myself. I just wanted another look at that face. But she was already some way off. All I could see was the back of her head. She was still singing. I didn't know what I'd seen. Lots of things must have rushed through my mind. Was it some kind of mask? Was it a trick of the light? I just had to have another look. "

" That was when I knew I seen a ghost. She'd gone. Vanished. That was it. "

" When I try to describe it, I can't ever get it quite right. No it wasn't like the blank face of a shop dummy. It was like a waxwork head before it's finished, but I can't say quite what was or wasn't there."

" But it's the tune that really haunts me. If I ever heard it again I'd know it straight away. It's like something you know but you've forgotten - like a song you used to sing at school. "

A Tower Of Strength

Whitton Tower, perched on the hillside half a mile above Rothbury, is now divided into private residential accommodation.

The 'toure and lytle barmekin' are mentioned in 1541, and the building appears on a list made in 1415. It is likely that Whitton was a fortified site a century earlier. The battlements are modern and the oldest sections of the building are the lowest. Whitton Tower is one of the finest peles in Northumbria with a barrel vaulted first floor and a stone lined dungeon. An upstairs room contained an alcove with an early carved piscina and a recess in the wall that may have been a priest hole.

The tower fell into ruin during the 17th. century but it was restored and extended by a succession of rectors. The best known of these was Canon Harcourt who held the living between 1822 and 1870. It was later bought by Sir Angus Watson who turned it into a hospital for children from Tyneside.

The Prince Of Wails

There is a tradition that Edward IV visited Whitton in May 1464. He had already earned a reputation as a soldier during his northern campaigns in the previous two years.

But it was conquest of a different kind that may have brought him to Whitton. It is said that the young king would travel many a mile to share the bed of a beautiful woman. Certainly Elizabeth Ogle of Whitton was well qualified in both looks and reputation. Could she have been the reason why Edward was conspicuously absent from the winning team at the Battle of Hexham on May 14th?

Despite the fact that his majesty shared the standards of morality of a jack rabbit, it's an unlikely encounter. The royal cup was already filled to overflowing with passion fruit cocktail.

The king was busy arranging a secret marriage to Elizabeth Woodville. The marriage - when disclosed - went down at court like vinegar spiced with digitalis. Lady Eleanor Butler, who was engaged to the king, called him a rat. Three of his mistresses, in a touching display of unity, locked their bedroom doors.

Powerful people were equally upset. The Earl of Warwick, who had lined up a French princess for the king, started raising an army. The Duke of Clarence and the Lancastrian faction also joined the opposition team. In 1469 Edward became Warwick's prisoner. The following year he fled to Holland. In 1470 Edward made a successful comeback and found a delightful new mistress - Jane Shore - a London goldsmith's wife, popularly known as Shore the Whore.

Despite this double success things were never quite the same again - partly, perhaps because of a certain irreverence that had become attached to the king's name. His notoriously noisy love making technique had earned him the nickname the Prince of Wails.

On winter nights, when the wind blows through the trees at the tower, a strange echoing sound has often been heard. It is perhaps only the most imaginative mind that would describe this sound as a scream of ecstasy, but it's enough to sustain the story of King Edward's encounter with Elizabeth Ogle in local folklore.

It also reinforces another tradition. Even if King Edward IV did visit Whitton Tower on that spring day in 1464, one can be pretty certain that he never slept there.

Another Folly

Sharpe's folly, close to Whitton Tower, was built as a kind of Victorian youth employment scheme.

It is said that Dr. Sharpe could view the sea from the summit. The trees that interrupt the view today make little difference. It has been unsafe to climb the tower for many years.

Following the road to Rothbury via Silverton Lane and Garleigh Bank you come to the Coquet Vale Hotel. This was Rothbury's original Railway Hotel - close to the end of the branch line.

The hotel is noted throughout the region for a warm welcome and fabulous food. The building is also home to a famous fertility chair* and a rather curious poltergeist.

Poltergeist In The Pipes?

Long serving hotel staff have commented on the way in which cellar switches seem to have a mind of their own. Lights and pumps will turn themselves on and off without human help. What is worse is that it always seems to happen when the hotel is particularly busy.

The new Railway Hotel, over the 15th. century Coquet Bridge, featured a startling poltergeist phenomenon in 1990.

Sharpe's Folly

A group of local musicians were enjoying a well earned break when a glass picked itself up from the table and emptied its contents over one of them. As if to prove this was no fluke, the poltergeist repeated the performance some minutes later.

The First Hooligan

The bridge itself may be linked to the world's first official hooligan.

Thomas Hullighan was a famous Rothbury resident who fought at one time or another for both sides in the English Civil Wars.

In more peaceful times he was a wheelwright who developed the trick of placing jagged rocks near to the Coquet Bridge - a ploy that was particularly effective around sunset.

The Coquet Bridge, Rothbury

The locals knew about this and took evasive action. Unsuspecting visitors however were unaware of the perils that lay ahead, but were grateful to the cheerful wheelwright who quickly repaired the damage for a modest fee.

Hullighan left Rothbury around the time of the Restoration. He met his end after a Newcastle drinking spree caused him to stagger under the wheels of a heavy carriage.

Other candidates for the eponym 'Hooligan' are the Chicago gangster Walter Hoolihan, and the London robber Patrick Hooligan. Patrick has the best claim through spelling. Walter wins hands down for dedication to villainy. But Rothbury's Thomas patented the title first, so this must give him the best claim of all.

An Arch Phantom

The pathside arch contains part of the oldest section of the bridge. Even on a warm summer's day people complain of an exaggerated feeling of cold when standing beneath the old stones. In pale moonlight the experience can be even more chilling.

The spectre that lurks here is a phantom feline. It is generally the hiss that commands the attention first. Your eyes scan the ground and you are relieved to see there is nothing more sinister than a large black cat sitting close to the stony rise of the arch.

What is odd is that the more the eyes concentrate on the feline form, the fainter it becomes. With a glance you are certain it is there, but a hard look is sure to make it vanish.

The phenomenon has been seen many times and it is always the same.   There is no recorded event that makes sense of it and no likely explanation has been offered.

The Best Meal In Northumbria?

The Corn Road restaurant, next to the Railway Hotel, is simply the very best in the region if you have time for a leisurely meal. It has been described as ' a little dolls' house of a restaurant with a wonderful cuisine.'

A Day At The Races

The building that is now the Corn Road dates from 1780. It's sited on Rattan Row, now Bridge Street, which runs south of the bridge made passable to 'heavy' vehicular traffic just 21 years earlier.   Wealthy landowners created the

The Best Little Restaurant in Northumbria

route in the 1830's. The corn was carried from Hexham to Alnmouth via Rothbury.

You can still see some of the old milestones on the modern roadside and in fields where the road used to be. The attractions of Rothbury, particularly the old racecourse, were a popular diversion for those who travelled the road.

Pie In The Sky

Today's Corn Road Restaurant is the likely former business address of another of Rothbury's blacker sheep.

In 1792 a gentleman called Thomas Pott took ship to Boston via Liverpool and Africa's slave coast. Mr. Pott had come from Elsdon to Rothbury to set up a pie making business two years earlier.

The success of the enterprise was short lived. Pott's pies were reputably tasty but they were hardly wholesome. Pott claimed they contained venison. Records unhappily do not reveal what was actually in them. His downfall came when one particular batch was reckoned to be the source of a local epidemic of food poisoning.

What happened during the next year is subject to speculation. The only formal charge recorded against a Thomas Pott was one of lewd and drunken behaviour. If this was the same man, we may suppose he left Rothbury pie-eyed. Whatever his condition was, it is certain that he left. In April 1792 he turns up in Liverpool with woman called Rachel, and a babe in arms.

Just ten years later Thomas Pott is listed amongst the 'Boston Aristocracy'. His good fortune was based on the dozen or more small shops he now owned. Thomas had gone into fashionable tableware, which explains his business slogan - 'Potts You Can Trust on Your Table.' This of course was more than could be said for the pies.

He retired in a condition of filthy richness around 1812, and lived long enough to see his son, Thomas Jnr., bribe his way to political office. Unfortunately Thomas Jnr's other vices included gambling and women. By the time his father died in 1819, the younger Pott had successfully frittered away most of the family fortune. In 1821 the last Pott's Emporium was sold. By 1824 Thomas Jnr. had been forced into gainful employment. He took the position of manager to a Mr. Cullin - the proprietor of Boston's most successful pie shop...

Potts Of Pennies

Thomas Pott promised to return to Rothbury after he had made his fortune.

This never happened, but an odd phrase was added to the local vocabulary that has been traced back to the reign of George IV. Whenever a coin was found in the street it was known as a 'Pott's penny'. One reason suggested for this is that Thomas Potts had returned, at least in spirit, and was flaunting his wealth by dropping coins wherever he went. This connection is unlikely. If there is a link to the pie man, the term was almost certainly ironic. A more likely alternative is perhaps a variant of 'a penny for the pot' - an expression used to suggest a small cash windfall.

Both these phrases passed out of regular usage before the end of the 19th. century.

The Hand On The Shoulder

Another possible Pott's connection comes from a phenomenon reported during the third and fourth decades of the 19th. century.

This was the 'hand on the shoulder' that was felt by people conducting their business on Rattan Row. What typically occurred was that somebody would be happily chatting away to a friend when they would feel a firm touch on the shoulder. They would turn round only to find nobody there.

The returning spirit of Thomas Pott's was mentioned as a possible culprit. The reason for this may have something to do with a kind of collective guilt felt by those responsible for driving him away.

The 'hand on the shoulder' has many parallels in haunting history. It has generally been dismissed as simple trickery, or as a symptom of hysteria.

The Saxon Cross

All Saints Parish Church is well worth a visit.

Much of the building was restored in the middle of the 19th. century. Only the chancel, its arch and the east wall of the south transept remain as evidence of 13th. century. construction.

The font pedestal is a part of the famous Rothbury Cross which was discovered when the nave was rebuilt. It is one of the finest examples of Saxon Christian carving. It dates from around AD 800.

One of its narrow faces includes writhing serpents gorging on their prey, whilst a naked figure struggles to escape the coils. The better of the broader faces is an Ascension scene.

Witches On The Hillside

Hillside West, high above Rothbury on the south side, is Rothbury's most prestigious address.

Towards the western extremity is Westfield House - once associated with a witches' coven.

Coquetdale has not earned the same reputation for witchcraft as some other corners of Northumbria, but it is known there were once several active covens. Some would have you believe that at least one is still in business today.

Following the B6341 westwards you come through a tree lined area on the approach to Thropton. This is best known today for red squirrels. Gallowfield Brae, on the left, once fulfilled the macabre function the name suggests.

Anger At The Cross Keys

Thropton's Cross Keys is a pleasant enough country hostelry, but it is perhaps best known for a high level of poltergeist activity.

In 1867 a local man, Douglas Moffat, had a bruising punch up with a visitor from Hexham, Frank Ford.

At first the matter seemed insignificant, but the battering Ford had taken slowly began to affect him. He walked unsteadily, his speech was slurred, and he became withdrawn and aggressive.

But he returned to Thropton regularly and would take up his favourite place in front of the fireplace at the hostelry. Sometimes he would stare for hours into the embers. At others he became loud and abusive and would throw glasses and plates at the wall.

The Cross Keys, Thropton

After a while the proprietor ran out of patience. Ford was banned from the pub for life. It is said that he took this very badly. The Cross Keys was the only place where he was ever truly happy.

A few months later he died at home in Hexham.

It was around the same time that plates and glasses started to fly at the Cross Keys. There were also serious problems with doors slamming and windows shattering.

Former landlord, Peter Hillier, reported various phenomena to the regional press in 1988. These included phantom footsteps, doors which opened and closed themselves, all sorts of unexplained rattlings, an electric kettle that boiled when it wasn't plugged in, an ashtray that shattered into tiny pieces, and a television that selected its own choice of viewing.

There have been many other similar reports over the years. Whatever is causing these aberrations is still very much on the active list.

A Famous Stronghold

The ruins of Hepple Tower can be seen to the left of the road as you enter the village.

The barony of Hepple was created by King John. The first baron was Ivo de Vesci who passed it jointly to two families - De Hepple and De Tailbois.

An early record (1372) shows how a Tailbois heir produced proof of his age - and right of inheritance - at Newcastle. Walter Hepple's godfather, Robert de Louthre, recalled that his own son was baptised the same day as the young heir. A second witness, John Lawson, said his son was buried at Rothbury on the same day.

This same Walter Tailbois was later taken prisoner by the Scots. An exchange was made for a Scottish prisoner 'with forty quarters of malt to boot'. By the 15th. century the tower was one of six belonging to Sir Robert Ogle. It was after a particularly devastating raid that the 'court' was temporarily transferred to Great Tosson.

An important incident in local history occurred just a short time before the union of 1603.

A 59 year old Hepple man, Robert Snowden, fought the Scottish champion, John Grieve. Both men were famous exponents of the killing power of the short sword. It was Grieve who came second after a fairly brief contest.

Snowden had little respect for the Scot even after his death. He cut off Grieve's sword arm and nailed it to a tree at Gamble Path near the head of the Coquet.

The Black Horse Rider

Hepple's most famous ghost sits proud and tall on the back of a black horse.

It is said that he returns to the village whenever there is a time of great danger. The greatest flood in modern times was the famous Fool's Day flood of 1992. In a similar deluge in 1912 Hepple Bridge was washed away.

The figure of a sturdy middle aged man on a black horse was seen on the far bank of the river warning people not to come close to the water's edge. The man was a stranger who seemed to have come from nowhere. One strange thing about him was that he had one hand permanently clasped to his stomach.

Murder At The Bothy

Robert Snowden, the master of the short sword, also had a black horse which he prized greatly.

The horse was stolen one night, but the sounds of disturbance woke Snowden and his guests. Two of them accompanied him as he pursued the thief to the border.

They were never far behind, and when they passed a primitive bothy near the roadside Snowden called out for the residents to identify themselves. He was answered by the neighing of his horse.

Snowden went to untie it, but as his hand struggled with the knot another hand came from beneath in the darkness. The long knife it held was plunged deep into Snowden's belly.

It was a tragic and bloody end to an illustrious career.

The Gallows Field

In former days the Lord of Hepple had the right to erect a gallows - a symbol of the power to make instant decisions about life and death. Many a moss trooper ended his days at the nearby Gibbet's Close.

There is some uncertainty about the exact site of the close. It is known it was placed in a field on the opposite side of the river. It is likely that this was Coates Hill which can be seen beneath the trees to the south of the road.

A Haunted Inn

Turn off the B6341 towards Holystone. The road winds through some delightful countryside on the way to the old village.

Holystone features the Lady's Well - with rather tentative religious and historical associations. There is also The Salmon Inn which was once very popular with visitors. Sadly The Salmon has shared the decline of many country pubs in recent years.

Even its famous selection of ghosts* seem to have joined the general pattern of lethargy in a community that was once a hive of activity.

The Yetlington Phenomenon

A mile beyond Sharperton Bridge at the top of the rise is the unusually named Light Pipe Cottage.

There are no ghosts here, but the story that unfolded during the early years of the 17th. century has all the features of the darkest gothic novel. It is also the kind of detective story that would defeat even the mind of the man from Baker Street.

300 years ago a lonely cottage stood in this area. It was the home of the celebrated Mary Yetlington.

12 year old Mary set off to visit friends in Harbottle on a summer's afternoon. Then she simply vanished, and despite many weeks of diligent searching no trace of the girl was found. It was rumoured she had been abducted by gipsies who had been seen in the area around the time of her disappearance.

Seven years later she returned. She had spent most of those years working as a servant to a clergyman in Newcastle. But her story of how it all began stretches credulity beyond the bounds of reason.

According to Mary she suddenly became weary on her walk and sat down under a tree. She had dozed off and in a dream-like state was transported through the air until she landed in the back of a tinker's cart on a road near Alston.

The tinker promised to take her home, but as the weeks went by it was clear he had no intention of releasing her. Finally she escaped from him near Consett, and hitched a lift with another traveller to Newcastle.

It was now that things went seriously wrong. Mary was caught up in a crowd, mistaken for a pickpocket, and locked in a prison dungeon with dozens of felons awaiting the visit of the assizes judge.

A chaplain visiting the prisoners heard the girl tell her story and was convinced she was mad. He persuaded the warden that because of her youth and mental state it would be wrong for her to face the summary justice of the court.

She was released subject to a legal bond that placed her in the care of a local clergyman. In effect it made her an unpaid servant until she was 21 years old. If she broke the terms of the bond, or tried to leave the parish, she could be hunted down as a criminal and made to answer for her original 'crime'.

Perhaps the threat was enough, or the experiences following her last 'escape' urged her to caution. We will never know. It was seven years later when she overheard a schoolmaster friend of the clergyman's talking about a proposed visit to Coquetdale. She persuaded him to check out her history with connections he had at Harbottle.

Three weeks later she was released from the bond and reunited with her family. Or was she?

Neighbours said that the new Mary Yetlington was quite unlike the girl who had vanished seven years earlier. The age was about right but other things seemed to be very wrong. The first Mary had fair hair ; the second was much darker. The first Mary had green eyes ; the second had blue. There were other things too. Seven years is a long time but this Mary seemed totally unfamiliar with her surroundings and the ways of the country.

But the family accepted her and were thrilled by her return Her story was never seriously questioned. In time she married, moved to a farm near Sharperton, had four children, and by all accounts a singularly unexceptional existence from that time on.

But the mysteries surrounding her disappearance and identity remain. Certainly we don't know the true story. The most plausible explanation is that the first Mary was abducted - possibly by gipsies - and then came into the dubious care of the tinker. A shorthand version of this suggests the tinker and gipsy are one and the same.

If there were two Mary Yetlingtons it is likely that something unpleasant happened to the first. Equally the second Mary must have known enough of the other's history to assume her identity. What the purpose of this was, or why the Yetlingtons were prepared to welcome this cuckoo in their nest are just two of the many odd facets of this case.

An Accident Of Birth

Harbottle is a delightfully sleepy village set at arguably the most attractive point of the Coquet Valley.

The name Harbottle derives from Here-Bottel - the station of an army. The castle, which is now greatly ruined, was once a mighty fortress. In 1296 it withstood an attack of 40,000 men under the command of Robert de Ros and the Earls of Athol and Menteith. In Tudor times it was the residence of Lord Dacre, Warden of the Middle Marches, who was one of the English heroes at Flodden.

Another event took place here that changed the course of history. Henry VIII's sister, Margaret, gave birth to a daughter, also named Margaret. This Margaret was the mother of Lord Darnley and grandmother to the Scottish King James VI, later to be also James I of England at the union of crowns in 1603.

The Not So Great Escape

In 1293 Thomas de Helm escaped from the castle but was captured as he sought sanctuary at Alwinton. Somehow he contrived to escape again and was captured at Simon Seth - probably Simonside. This time his captors were taking no chances. It is said that 'his head was removed by eight sturdy blows' - obviously the work of a trainee or amateur axeman. This grisly trophy was displayed, for the edification of all, on Harbottle gibbet.

Mystic Rites

Above Harbottle is the famous Drake Stone - associated with ancient rites and ceremonial.*

Split Level

The church of St. Michael and All Angels at Low Alwinton is worth a visit.

Old tombstones form the footpath and other headstones include the locally popular skull and crossbones.

The church itself is an unusual. It is built on a slope with the altar at the highest point, and the chancel above the nave.

The Ancient Clennel Hall

The Reivers Return

Clennel Street was once the most famous of the 'thieves rodes'. The hall, which incorporates a pele tower, is first mentioned in the border survey of 1541 as ' the property of Percival Clennel, gent, newly reparelled and brattyshed by the same Percival.'

Bratticing was an important part of the defence system. It was a kind of wooden staging built to stick out beyond the parapet. Loopholes were strategically placed so that the foot of the walls could been seen. Later, stronger, designs placed the loopholes especially to facilitate the dropping of stones or other missiles onto the heads of unwelcome visitors.

It is not known how old the pele tower is. The earliest well worn date stone is usually read as 1365.

A report of 1541 said it was impossible to encourage people to live in this area because of the regular Scots raids. The tower contains a reivers' dungeon. Regular hangings took place on a conveniently sturdy old oak near the hall.

Rob's Ride

A phantom associated with the hall is a heavily armed horseback rider known only as Rob.

Tradition has it that he rides to the hall and, without dismounting, bangs loudly on the door with the base of his sword.

If the door is opened, he vanishes immediately. If not, he sets about pummelling the woodwork with a heavy war axe until it is opened to him.

As there are no obvious signs of such savage treatment to the present doors it is assumed that Rob is at least temporarily redundant.

Taking The High Road

Take the high road by Low Alwinton church towards Netherton. As you mount the rise it is worth pulling off the road for a moment for the superb views over the Cheviots.

You pass Wilkinson Park on the right and Newton farmhouses at the top of the hill. Biddlestone quarry can be seen ahead.

The road drops steeply towards Biddlestone. Just less than half a mile beyond the Home Farm complex you reach some woods. Park near the carefully concealed track on the left.

The path leads up gently to an old Roman Catholic chapel. It is now surrounded by conifers which heighten the feeling of isolation. There are blasted trees in front of the building which is now sealed.

The chapel was once a pele tower that belonged to the Selby family. In 1796 the family built their mansion to the south and converted the tower into a chapel.

A secret passage exists - built into the thickness of the walls. It is likely that this passage has seen service as a priest hole.

The Muffled Voice

Visitors to the chapel - particularly around sunset - have commented on a strange phenomenon. It seems that a high pitched but indistinct voice seems to call from inside the chapel walls.

Some say this is the wind in the trees, or the shrill evening chatter of birds. Others say it is a voice that will not be silenced until a second hidden passage reveals a horrific secret...

* Featured in Ghost Trails of Northumbria

No. 5
Town &
Country

This linear walking and motoring tour
takes approximately six hours

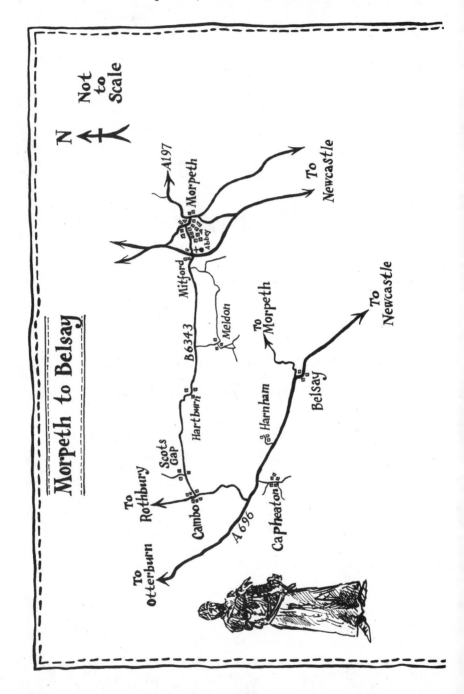

Morpeth to Belsay

N

Not to Scale

A197

Morpeth

To Newcastle

Abbey

Mitford

Meldon

To Morpeth

B6343

Harnham

Hartburn

Belsay

To Newcastle

Scots Gap

To Rothbury

Cambo

A696

Capheaton

To Otterburn

This final trail explores some of the lesser known, but nevertheless fascinating, corners of Northumbria.

Morpeth's original parish church of St. Mary the Virgin is situated some way from the main part of the town on the A197.

Bridegroom Tolls

The walled gateway is a memorial to HR Fenwick of Netherton who died in 1861. There has been a local custom for bridegrooms to pay a toll as they passed through the arch on their wedding day.

The inscription reads : ' Wake thou that sleepest and arise from the dead. Christ shall give thee light.'

A Grisly Business

Resurrectionists of a different kind were a menace during the 18th. and 19th. centuries. The huge churchyard at St. Mary's made it a popular target.

The grave robbers normally worked in teams of four. Two handled the spades and the others operated as lookouts.

Bodies were looted for valuables, but the primary objective was the sale of the corpse itself. The demand for cadavers for dissection was enormous and money changed hands on a 'no questions asked' basis. Body snatching reached epidemic proportions when the legitimate supply of corpses dried up after the Napoleonic Wars.

The Watch Tower

The value of a cadaver declined the longer it remained in the ground. Fresh graves were always the most likely to be attacked. At the height of the grisly trade the families of the deceased would often organise a watch for the first few weeks after interment.

At St. Mary's they found another solution. A watchtower - really a hut behind the church - was built by public subscription in 1831. Here a fire was lit for the guards who mounted regular patrols around the churchyard.

The Runaway Corpse

But for a while at least the attacks continued. The most popular hour to strike was just before dawn. There are many macabre stories associated with the body-snatchers.

One concerns a baker who was walking by the churchyard with his basket on his shoulder. Suddenly a corpse appeared to leap over the wall in front of him.

He dropped his basket and ran away screaming, " Help! Help! They're getting away."

A More Comfortable Posture

Both guards and robbers became hardened against the sights they experienced.

One famous night a gang of snatchers were working in near darkness and pulled out the wrong coffin from a family grave. They realised their mistake when the coffin crumbled and a putrefied corpse slithered out.

Not to be deterred, they propped the corpse up against a convenient gravestone and continued their search for the right box.

In the pale light of dawn a guard patrol found the rotted corpse still in its seated position.

One guard turned to his companion and said : " I reckon he got weary of all that lying down."

The Finest Glass

The church is one of the largest and most interesting in Northumbria. The east window features some rare medieval stained glass. The aisles, nave and tower all date from the 14th. century.

Thomas Telford

Morpeth's Telford bridge also dates from 1831. It is an example of the work of the most famous civil engineer of his age. Thomas Telford who was also responsible for roads, canals, and the famous Menai suspension bridge.

An Evil Attack

Some years ago a man named Turnbull was employed as a cash carrier. After walking down the hill from Hepscott he rested on a bench near the corner of Bridge Street. His attacker came from a nearby park and crept up behind him before cutting his throat.

Turnbull managed to hang on to the money and staggered to the Waterford Inn nearby to raise the alarm. Although he lost a lot of blood the wound was superficial. The prompt ministrations of a local doctor saved his life.

There have been a number of reports of 'phantom' attacks in the same area. Some people imagine they have been grabbed from behind either by the hair or the throat. Never has the 'attacker' been visible, and never has the 'victim' come to any harm.

Walk along Bridge Street past the Vanburgh town hall and continue across Oldgate. Low Stanners is the grassy area upstream from the new bridge.

A Brace Of Villains

In September 1821 a pair of notorious villains were hung at this spot. One was John Wilkinson who had a fairly late start to a life of crime. At the age of 30 he had risen to a position of some responsibility at St. Hilda's pit in South Shields. He was entrusted with the men's wages.

The temptation proved too much for him. He stole a week's colliery pay and went to Newcastle to spend as much as he could. Although he was soon arrested the evidence was inconclusive and he was released.

But his workmates delivered their own justice. Wilkinson was stripped, tarred and feathered and thrown into a pond. He survived this ordeal and moved to Sunderland where he became the leader of an organised criminal gang.

He was arrested again for highway robbery - a crime he had carried out with others on the Ponteland Road. This time the evidence was strong. The jury found him guilty.

But his trials were not yet over. Another charge had been brought for a robbery the previous April. Standing in the dock with him this time was William Hetherington, a former sailor.

The two men had committed many robberies together. The charge they now faced was for a vicious attack on a Longbenton farmer called William Nesbit. The unfortunate man had been pulled from his horse, beaten and robbed.

Previous witnesses against Wilkinson and Hetherington had been intimidated, but Nesbit stood his ground and made a positive identification. The two men were sentenced to hang.

On the day before the execution their accomplice in the Nesbit attack - a man called Maddison - was reprieved. Wilkinson and Hetherington enjoyed a few hours of hope that their sentences would be commuted to life imprisonment.

It was not to be.

The hanging drew a large crowd. Many were disappointed in the spectacle. The executioner had tied his knots too well. It was all over in just a manner of minutes.

The Witch Pricker

Public executions were only slightly less popular than public humiliations.

The famous Scottish witchfinder, Kincaid, visited Morpeth on two occasions during the 1690's. Northumberland was technically beyond his sphere of jurisdiction but he happily acted as a paid advisor to the court.

The favoured method was to strip the victim, blindfold her, and then search her body for some area of hard skin. The pin was then carefully inserted. If the woman did not cry out, or the mark start to bleed, she was instructed to find the pin herself. If her hand moved to the wrong part of her body it was said that the devil had touched the area around the pin. This was sufficient evidence to convict her as a witch.

The Morpeth Ordeal

Nathaniel Webster, a magistrate, gave this account of what he saw one July day in Morpeth :

" There were three (women) brought out. I could tell from their wretched condition they had been ill used. They held (their) hands to (their) faces."

" Kincaid spoke with his assistant, with (the) matron and priest some way apart. At his (Kincaid's) bidding the women were stripped. The crowd pushed on but were held by the militia."

" The other man (Kincaid's assistant) took up the pricking. He made examination of the older (women) first but they had small interest for him. Presently he sought the youngest - a girl of 15. (To) no avail did she stave (off) his hand. The rope held her limbs."

" At first he found nothing. Then (he) instructed that the hurdle be turned. At this the girl began to scream. The matron put a muslin to her mouth."

" As he took the instrument, the crowd fell silent. He put it to her flesh and the muslin was (taken) off. The girl made great lamentation. The rope was loosed. Her hand sought the instrument which she plucked."

" Kincaid came (forward) and declared she bled. This was certain (proof that) the girl was no witch for Satan is guardian of his mark."

" The women (were) yielded up to their own (families). Kincaid   declared (to the crowd) there was no witch in Morpeth. They cheered him."

The Witchfinders

There are few accounts of witchfinding as dispassionate as Webster's. To many the pricking was a spectator event and the witchfinder knew how to play to the crowd. Their mood often determined his verdict.

The question of blood flowing from the mark is a complex one. It is known that some of the pricking tools were designed with retractable points. If the point did not enter the flesh there is no blood but apparent 'evidence' that the victim was a witch.

There are few doubts that the trauma of the ordeal could induce a state of shock. This could be enough for the victim to be unaware that the instrument had been used. It is also possible that acupuncturist principles could apply, or even that trauma itself can affect blood flow. It is also believed that hypnotism was sometimes applied to the victims.

The witchfinders were amongst the most evil men of their era. They fed on public ignorance and fear and used 'professional' con tricks to make arbitrary decisions about life and death.

The women who faced Kincaid in Morpeth three centuries ago were   fortunate to suffer no more than pain, abuse and humiliation. He was not always so generous.*

Fountain's Daughter

Newminster Abbey is close to the bridge on the B6348. A public footpath leads along a private drive. When the tree lined path swings right fragments of walls can be picked out together with remains of an archway and the arcades of three sides of the cloisters.

Newminster was founded in 1137 as the daughter house of the famous Fountains Abbey in Yorkshire. A year later Newminster was attacked and ravaged by the Scots. It was rebuilt and became powerful until the monasteries were dissolved by Henry VIII.

A Phantom Rabbit?

There are stories of dogs chasing a rabbit towards the ruined archway. By all accounts the dogs invariably pull up short of the arch itself and set up a terrible howling.

Setting aside the possibility of a phantom bunny, there's a possible link here to reports of a 'strange oppressive atmosphere' noted by visitors to the ruin.

Visions of a 'white monk', or 'white lady' date from more than two centuries ago. This apparently androgynous creature has not put in an appearance in recent years.

King John's Revenge

Follow the B6343 to Mitford, go through the first part of the village, turn left downhill and park near the River Wansbeck.

Mitford Church

The village was burnt by King John in 1216 as part of his reprisals policy. It is likely that much of the original church was destroyed at the same time but there are Norman fragments dating from 1135. The building was substantially restored during the 19th. century. The south arcade, the chancel and transepts survive from 13th. and 14th. centuries.

There are some 11th. century stone coffins outside and an unusual priest's doorway which was once part of the main building.

By the north wall of the chancel there is the worn effigy and tomb of Bertram Reveley with it's unusual epitaph :

' Bertram to us so dutiful a son. If more were fit it should for thee be done.'

Although the precise meaning of this was obvious when it was carved in 1622, modern readers not surprisingly have difficulty with it.

Jack The Ghosthunter

The late Reverend Jack Richardson had a long association with the   church.

Jack himself enjoyed a number of ' incarnations' as sailor, vicar, college teacher and writer. He was very good at all of them. Those who knew him talk of an exceptional and kindly man with a complex and lively character.

As a ghosthunter Jack was one of the best. Even in his later years he still followed phantoms with great alacrity. He even found them in the most unlikely places - such as the Welbeck Library of Northumberland College of Arts and Technology.

Jack believed passionately in the phantom world. To him this was as matter of fact as the roses in his garden or the wordprocessor he kept in the toilet. He had the unnerving habit of casually informing friends and visitors to his home that a spirit was present.

The Bridge & Castle at Mitford

An brief account of his exorcism of the troubled spirit of Kate Babbington can be found near the end of this chapter.

An Unfortunate Family

The castle is accessed from a stile by the road bridge. Follow the riverside path briefly, then turn uphill.

The principal ruins are those of the five sided keep. It was built around 1138 by William Bertram but destroyed about 80 years later. It was rebuilt and in time became the property of the Mitford family. They abandoned it in the early 17th. century, preferring the more comfortable manor house nearby.

The most unfortunate owner of the castle of Aymer de Valence, Earl of Pembroke. It was said that in his family no father ever lived to see his son. Aymer broke the tradition. He was killed at a tournament organised to celebrate his wedding.

A Wicked Man And A Cunning Plan

After Bannockburn Northumbria was overrun by the Scots. Many of the leading barons felt it prudent to come to an accommodation with their traditional enemies. Sometimes this meant allowing the men from the north easy access to valuable looting sites - often the property of local rivals.

Sir Gilbert de Middleton, Warden of the March, went even further. He filled the Mitford dungeons with as many of his neighbours as they could hold. Then he demanded huge ransoms.

Sir Gilbert went to some trouble to secure a potentially valuable prize. After three days of riding be captured Louis de Beaumont, the bishop elect of Durham, at Rushyford. An extra bonus of this attack was the capture of the bishop's brother. In order to guard these assets well Gilbert imprisoned the bishop at Morpeth and kept his brother at Mitford.

The ransoms were raised by William de Felton. He visited the castle to inform Sir Gilbert that the money was ready. The porters he sent out to fetch it were quietly ambushed by Felton's hit squad. In order to prevent any possibility of the alarm being raised the squad obeyed Felton's orders to the letter. Each of the unfortunate porters had his throat cut.

At a given signal a second Felton squad, hidden outside the castle walls, stormed in through the open gates. A few minutes later a surprised Sir Gilbert was himself a prisoner. Felton hastily despatched him with an armed guard to London. Gilbert de Middleton was tried for his crimes, found guilty, and was executed.

The Warrior Ghost

The castle ghost is a fearsome spectacle. A grizzled old warrior is said to leap from behind the stones waving a great sword in one hand and holding the head of his latest victim in the other. The head, rather than the warrior, lets out a terrible warning scream.

Meldon Church

Nobody is sure quite what happens next. The two boys who reported the phenomenon in 1934 did not hang around long enough to find out...

A Blinking Statue

Meldon provides a stark contrast to Mitford. It is a remote windswept place.

The churchyard is entered through a wrought iron gate that closes viciously. There is a fine example of the skull and crossbones carved on a gravestone near the church entrance.

The recumbent effigy of William Fenwick is noted in local folklore because it is supposed to blink. From the historian's point of view there is probably more interest in the well preserved detail of clothing.

More curious than the blink is the question of dates. The tomb records Fenwick's date of demise as 1659. The window dedicated to his memory is dated 1652.

Grave Matters

The famous Meg o' Meldon is also closely associated with the church. Meg is best remembered for the treasure that remains hidden somewhere nearby in a dark corner of a long secret tunnel.*

Ghost In The Road

The minor road rejoins the B6343 on the way to Hartburn. A dip in the road over the bridge on the run into the village is the popular sighting place of a familiar phantom.

On many occasions motorists have taken evasive action at this point when they see a white lady in the roadway. There is never any impact and the 'phantom' vanishes almost as soon as it is seen.

In common with similar accounts from around the country this 'phantom' is almost certainly an illusion created by stream mist.

The History Man

St. Andrew's Church is again Norman in origin but largely rebuilt in the 13th. century. It contains a monument to John Hodgson, arguably the county's greatest historian.

A gravestone near the door features a rather unusual crossbones and angels combination. The 15 names on one stone near the gate may set some kind of record.

Fragments of Roman masonry by the north wall are visible proof of an important connection. The famous Devil's Causeway - one of the northernmost road arteries of the Roman Empire - ran through Hartburn.

The Missing Legion

In AD 126 the Fifth Legion set off to march from Corbridge to Hartburn. Despite the lack of evidence of a fight, and the unlikelihood of mass defection, they have still not arrived.

It is a mystery that has been turned to time and time again by writers and scholars but no satisfactory explanation has emerged.

A Delightful Walk

A footpath leads down through ancient woodland to the Hart Burn. The delightful short walk along the burn is one of the best kept secrets of Northumbria.

One deep pool is the place where a baker's chest was lowered into the water to conceal valuables from Viking raiders.

The Doctor Of Decorum

Then there is Doctor Sharpe's grotto. You can still see clearly where a passageway was constructed underground that leads to a large cave shelter.

By all accounts the Hartburn lads of the 19th. century were a lusty lot. They would lie in wait for hours for a glimpse of the local girls running from their shelter to bathe in the stream. The Reverend soon put a sharp stop to it. He created an underground passage from the grotto shelter - which served as a changing room - so that the ladies 'could enter the water without the impertinent eye of idle curiosity'.

The Dragon's Den

Following the burn beyond the woods brings you to the Dragon's Den. The legendary dragon had a taste for young ladies that went beyond a spying mission at the bathing pool.

Eventually the local men registered their displeasure by killing him. This all too common attitude to dragons probably explains why they were already on the endangered species list even in far off mythical times.

A Model Village

Cambo was created by the wealthy Trevellyan family for workers at their 20 square mile Wallington Estate. Wallington Hall is one of the least inspiring of the great houses of Northumbria for the visitor, but Cambo does its best to make up for the disappointment.

The village is situated on high ground about a mile to the north of Wallington. It is a little gem that combines many of the better features of functional architecture and design. It was laid out as a model village in 1740. The cottage rows are nicely spaced with a natural symmetry focused around the village green and fountain.

The school attended by Launcelot 'Capability' Brown,* the famous landscape gardener, is now the reading room. The delightful post office shop is based on a pele tower.

The Fountain, Cambo

The shop used to be run by a warlock. At that time the ground floor was used as a cattle shed, and an exterior staircase led to the first floor shop.

Many years ago, former owner George Handyside said :

" My father and grandfather had this shop before me, and before that it was kept by a warlock. People didn't dare owe him anything. There was a woman who lived where our kitchen is now and she kept a cow. When she churned she locked the door for fear the warlock cast an evil eye on the milk and turned it sour. His shop was upstairs. That's his window that's walled up."

Little more is known about him but it is believed the local meaning of warlock is better interpreted as wizard. George Handyside believed the man was still alive in 1818 when the pele tower was altered to make it habitable.

The present owners have experienced no problems with sour milk.

A Gothic Monstrosity

The church features a massive tower which is a prominent landmark. The building is a 19th. century monstrosity which cynical locals will tell you was built for the greater glory of the Trevellyan family. Many of them are buried in the churchyard.

The Phantom Flower Fetcher

During the closing years of the 19th. century a local woman used to bring flowers every Sunday to place on certain graves.

After her death the locals were surprised that the flowers continued to appear regularly. Nobody ever saw who brought them and there was inevitable speculation about a phantom flower fetcher.

The flower deliveries eventually became intermittent and stopped altogether around the time of the First World War.

The Roman Hoard

Turn off the B6342 to join the A696. There is a brief detour for Capheaton.

The village is connected to the main road by Silver Lane. This takes its name from a rich hoard of Roman coins and plate found by workmen in 1749.

The men quietly sold the coin and some of the plate before giving the rest to Sir John Swinburne, the lord of the manor.

Sir John managed to recover some of the stolen property from silversmiths in Newcastle. The collection is now in the British Museum.

Catnap In France

The magnificent hall is not open to the public.

The first Swinburnes settled here in 1294. The first baronet was Sir John Swinburne. As a boy he mysteriously disappeared and turned up in a French monastery. When he came home questions were asked about his identity. He convinced the doubters by describing the markings of a cat that still lived in the house.

The Jacobite Connection

The tragic Third Earl of Derwentwater is also associated with the hall. He was a Jacobite leader who was captured and executed after the siege of Preston.*

More Secret Passages

The Swinburnes were the most prominent catholics in the region. They were involved in many of the plots and intrigue of the 17th. and 18th. centuries.

Given the constant uncertainties of those times it is hardly surprising that Capheaton Hall featured seven hiding places. Two of these were typical priest holes in the chapel at the top of the house. The most ingenious was a false chimney section covered in stone slating.

The Phantom Piper

Capheaton's most famous ghost is the phantom piper. He said to appear at times of danger and to rouse the villagers from their beds with a rousing skirl.

There are reports of this happening as a warning of fire in 1783, and again in 1821. It is said that the most recent appearance came just before the first German bombers appeared overhead during the early months of the Second World War. This performance was perhaps unnecessary. No bombs fell close to Capheaton.

The Gated Road

Rejoin the A696. The gated road leading to Harnham is a left turn three miles to the south.

The hamlet is built on a distinctive rocky spur. The roadside complex of farm buildings is now a Buddhist monastery.

Lovely Kate

Harnham Hall is an elegant building that incorporates the tower of the Swinburnes. In 1667 the estate passed to the Babingtons. The best known member of this family was the celebrated Kate.

The tomb is on private land. Permission to visit should be obtained from the hall.

Follow the wall to the left of the hall. Go through the gate, turn down left. The empty vault can be seen in an opening in the high wall on the right. It contains a rocky shelf where the coffin once rested and an inscribed board :

' Here lyeth the body of Madam Babington, who was laid in this sepulchre on 9th. September, 1670.

My time is past, as now you see, I viewed the dead as you do me. Or' long
you'll be as low as I, And some will look on thee.'

The famous inscription on the wall reads :

In hopes of future bliss, contented here I lie
Tho I would have been pleased to live, Yet was not displeased to die.
For life has ts comforts and sorrows too.
For which to the Lord of heaven, our most grateful thanks are due.
If it were otherwise, our hopes would rest, Where nature tells us we cannot be
blest, How for my hopes are vain are founded well, God only knows but the last
day will tell.

Kate Babington was the beauty of her time. When she visited Durham large
crowds gathered to look at her. The local magistrates, concerned about the crush
in the streets, issued a strange bye law.

' Whensoever Dame Katherine Babington shall have cause to enter a   cook's
shop, she must not eat sixpenny pies in public, but (rather) in a private room,
that she be not stared at by the people'.

Kate was a non-conformist with a dislike for both the personality and ideology
of the Vicar of Bolam. She was also a supporter of Cromwell. It was with the
authority of the Lord Protector that she arranged for the vicar to be literally
'pulled from his pulpit'.

But the political wheel turned. Soon after the Restoration the vicar returned to
his living. Kate was excommunicated.

In 1670 she became ill. Some days before she died she studied her still
beautiful face in a mirror. Then she scratched these words on the window pane in
her room :

' Vain is the work of a man. Omnia Vanitas'. (All is Vanity)

It was a theme taken up by her contemporary John Bunyan. In his   landmark
epic, Pilgrim's Progress, published in 1675, he makes much of 'Vanity Fair'.
This is more than coincidence. Thackeray's masterpiece of the same name (
published in 1847) continued the tradition. Kate Babington's few words have
almost certainly been the source of much inspiration. Kate died in August 1670.
For ten days her husband argued for the right to bury her in consecrated ground.
The vicar refused. The special tomb was carved from the rock in the garden and
she was buried there.

Some years later the lead of her coffin was stolen by gipsies and the bones were
exposed. A new coffin was made but the tomb is now empty.

The late Reverend Jack Richardson conducted a special service of exorcism for Kate. He was aware of what he called her 'restless wanderings' and believed that his ministrations had helped.

Jack was a regular visitor to this unusual vault. He felt the presence of Kate Babington intensely. He was able to sense her troubled spirit. Following the exorcism many have reported a changed mood and atmosphere around the vault. It seems now, after more than three centuries, the story of Kate Babington is finally over.

𝕿𝖍𝖊 𝕭𝖔𝖓𝖓𝖞 𝕷𝖆𝖘𝖘

The final leg of this trail follows the A696 to Belsay.

The so called Bonny Lass of Belsay is a ghostly temptress.

With the wink of an eye and the swish of a skirt she is said to tempt young men to follow her for miles. When they come too close or pause to look too long she vanishes.

It has been said that the ghost is the spirit of a wealthy Newcastle merchant's daughter called Carolyn, or possibly Caroline. What became of the woman and why she should haunt the area - especially around the lake near Belsay Crag - is not known.

Early in the 18th. century a young woman called Carolyn was thrown from her horse near Bolam Lake. She died almost instantly as her skull was shattered on rocks. Some say this is Carolyn, the ghostly temptress.

Of all the ghost stories of Northumbria this is the most frequently recurring. Reported sightings of the Bonny Lass of Belsay, also known as the Belsay Silkie, are remarkably common. They occur regularly towards sunset during the warmer months.

If the serious ghosthunter is seeking a challenge, this can hardly be it...

* See Ghost Trails of Northumbria

Historical Notes

BANNOCKBURN, BATTLE OF In June 1314 Edward II (qv) led an army of 20,000 men to relieve Stirling Castle. Robert the Bruce (qv) intercepted them with a much smaller force and the English came second.

'CAPABILITY' BROWN, LAUNCELOT (1715 - 83) English landscape gardener who revolutionised garden and parkland layout in the 1700's. He designed or remodelled nearly 150 estates including the gardens at Blenheim and Kew. He worked to achieve casual effects, with scattered groups of trees and gently rolling hills. He earned his nickname from a habit of saying that a place was 'capable of improvement'.

CHARLES I, KING OF GREAT BRITAIN (1625 - 1649 B. 1600) Lack of honesty, political foresight, military and administrative competence and marriage to a Catholic princess led to civil war (qv), in which he came second, and a date with an axeman in Whitehall. Unfortunate as it might have been for him, his death was the ultimate saviour of the Monarchy in Britain as it divided the parliamentarians.

CIVIL WAR, THE ENGLISH (1642 - 1651) More properly called the Civil Wars. The culmination of the deterioration in the relationship between the crown and the parliament through the reigns of James I and Charles I (qv) , and the financial and religious policies of Charles in particular, triggered rebellion in Scotland and Ireland. The short and long parliaments of 1640 demanded reform which included parliamentary control over the king's choice of advisors. In January 1642 Charles failed to secure the arrest of five members of parliament and quit the capital. He set up his standard at Nottingham in August of the same year. The royalists enjoyed early success in battles at Edgehill, Newcastle and Hopton, but failed to consolidate these victories. Scottish troops under Argyll entered England and contributed to the first parliamentary success at Marston Moor. Argyll's troops were withdrawn to deal with a royalist uprising in Scotland and an indecisive battle was fought at Newbury.

In 1645 Fairfax's New Model Army inflicted a major defeat on the royalists at Naseby. In 1648 revolts in the south anticipated further intervention by the Scots on the king's behalf. Fairfax crushed the rebellion in the south and Cromwell defeated the invading Scots at Preston. Charles was tried by a court set up by the Rump Parliament and executed on 30th. January 1649. In 1650 Cromwell inflicted a final defeat on the Scots at Dunbar, and in the following year Charles II's invading army was crushed at Worcester. The Commonwealth formed to govern the country at the end of the war lasted until Booth's Rising and the Restoration of 1660.

COLLINGWOOD, CUTHBERT, Ist BARON (1759 - 1810) born in Newcastle upon Tyne, he joined the navy at the age of 11 and rose to the rank of Admiral. He fought outstandingly during the Napoleonic Wars and took over from Nelson after the latter's death at Trafalgar.

DERWENTWATER, JAMES RADCLIFFE, 3rd EARL OF (1689 - 1716) Brought up in the French court as companion to James Stuart, the Old Pretender, he returned to England in 1710 to live on his English estates. He joined in the rebellion of 1715, but escaped arrest through the devotion of his tenants. In October 1715, he joined Tom Forster at Greenrigg and together they went to Preston where the Jacobites lost a battle and the Earl was captured. He was beheaded on Tower Hill in February 1716.

DOUGLAS, ARCHIBALD, 4th EARL OF (1369? - 1424) Unlucky in his encounters with the English, he was captured and ransomed twice, only to be killed in France by the Duke of Bedford.

EDWARD III, KING OF ENGLAND (1327-1377 b.1312) Began his reign by imprisoning his mother and executing her lover, Roger de Mortimer. Militarily unsuccessful in Scotland, he turned his attention to France, started the Hundred Years War, and promptly lost, despite the brilliancy at Crecy, Calais and Poitiers. Since he was so occupied with military matters, his reign saw a significant increase in the role of Parliament.

EDWARD IV (1461 - 1470, 1471 - 83. Born 1442.) A brave and popular soldier during the Wars of the Roses. He won a significant victory at Towton (1461), but his marriage to Elizabeth Woodville alienated his mentor, Warwick the Kingmaker (qv). He was driven into exile but returned to lead a successful campaign in March 1471. He gave England domestic peace but failed to reconcile disputes at court. The most important of these, between the Woodvilles and the Duke of Gloucester (the future Richard III) caused further strife after his death.

GREY, CHARLES, 2nd EARL (1764 - 1845) British Prime Minister from 1830 to 1834, it was under his administration that the first Reform Bill was passed. It is his monument that overlooks Grey Street & Grey's Square in Newcastle and after whom the tea is named. He fell out of favour with the Hanoverian kings after declaring that the monarchy should demonstrate its fitness to govern.

HENRY VIII (1509 - 47. Born 1491) Henry came to the throne with little political or governmental experience. He learned these skills quickly and presided over one of the most lavish and cultured courts in Europe. His decision to divorce Catherine of Aragon created a division with Rome and the establishment of the Church of England. He was always the final power in government but had little taste for administration. This was left to famous servants, notably the three Thomas' - More, Cromwell, and Wolsey - all of whom suffered considerably after falling from the king's favour. Henry is now best remembered for his six wives and as the composer of Greensleeves.

HOTSPUR, SIR HENRY PERCY. (1364 - 1403) Son of the Earl of Northumberland, Hotspur was particularly zealous in guarding the borders. Captured by the Scots at Otterburn (1388), he later helped Henry IV to the throne, won a victory for him at Homildon Hill (1402), but changed sides and died at the Battle of Shrewsbury (1403). Hotspur, who has near legendary status in Northumberland, was portrayed as a contemporary of Prince Henry (later Henry V) by Shakespeare. He was in fact 23 years older than the prince. But the near sibling rivalry between the two 'young men' is an important theme in Henry IV Part One. Shakespeare climaxes the play with Prince Hal locked in mortal combat with Hotspur on the battlefield. The fatal blow provokes the words - ' Oh Harry! Thou hast robbed me of my youth.' Hotspur was killed a few months before his 40th. birthday.

JACOBITES is the name given to the supporters of the deposed James II (VII of Scotland) and his son, James. Jacobite plots began in 1688, but the first serious threat to the Hanoverian succession came in 1715. This was the Earl of Mar's Scottish rising, which was supported by Northumberland's Thomas Forster and the Earl of Derwentwater. The rebels reached Preston where they capitulated.

The more serious affair was in 1745. 'Bonnie Prince Charlie' had landed in Scotland two years previously with 10,000 French troops. The standard was raised at Glenfinnan in '45 and support came mainly from the west and central highlands. The prince captured Perth and Edinburgh, and a victory at Prestonpans encouraged him to march into the heart of England. The expected support did not materialise and the prince turned back at Derby. There was a last victory at Falkirk before the slaughter of the highlanders at   Culloden Moor. Prince Charles escaped with his life, but the Jacobite cause was lost.

JAMES VI & I, KING OF SCOTLAND (1567 - 1625) KING OF GREAT BRITAIN (1603 - 1625 b. 1566) Became King at a very tender age when his mother, Mary, Queen of Scots, was forced to abdicate. His father, Darnley having been murdered with his mother's connivance, James was left in the care of a variety of Scottish nobles. A shrewd and flexible diplomat, James managed to tame the wilder excesses of his nobles and keep the church in check also. Hailed as a great King of Scotland, his reputation as a king in   England after his accession to the throne was decidedly dodgy. He was seen as a drunken, foul mouthed, undignified coward with homosexual leanings. His financial irresponsibility, pro Spanish foreign policy and continuous assertions of royal authority, led to a deterioration of relations between Parliament and the monarchy which led ultimately to the execution of his son, Charles I.

JOHN, KING OF ENGLAND (1199 - 1216 b. 1167) Younger brother of Richard the Lionheart (qv) he was Regent in his brother's absence. Not content with succeeding to the throne of England, he renewed the war with France and lost most of the English possessions there. His objections to the Pope's nomination for Archbishop of Canterbury led to his excommunication in 1212. His objections to the power of his barons led to Magna Carta in 1215. Not so much the monster portrayed by history as a weak and stubborn man, with a cruel streak.

RICHARD I, 'THE LIONHEART' (1189 - 1199. Born 1157) A son of Henry II, he spent only 6 months of his reign in England, preferring his French castles when he wasn't away at the Crusades. His brother, John, was Regent in his absence and tried to take the throne for himself.

ROBERT THE BRUCE, KING OF SCOTLAND (1306 - 1329, B. 1274) After swearing allegiance to Edward I, changed his mind and made a bid for an independent Scottish kingdom. Conducted a guerilla war and used scorched-earth tactics until finally he inflicted a crushing defeat on Edward II at Bannockburn (qv). He only got his heart's desire after the death of Edward II, when both the English and the Pope finally accepted Scottish independence.

THACKERAY, WILLIAM MAKEPEACE (1811 - 1863) English novelist, comic illustrator and journalist who wrote many novels, including, in 1848, Vanity Fair.

TELFORD, THOMAS (1757 - 1834) Scottish civil engineer extraordinaire, he built bridges, canals, docks, harbours waterways and roads. His most notable achievements are possibly the 177m long Menai Bridge connecting Anglesey with mainland Wales and the Caledonian Canal, connecting the east and west coasts of Scotland.

WARWICK, RICHARD NEVILLE, EARL OF, 'THE KINGMAKER' (1428-1471) Great statesman and soldier of the period. Sided initially with the Yorkists during the Wars of the Roses, his capture of Henry VI helped put Edward IV (qv) on the throne, behind which Richard Neville was definitely the power. Losing influence and power, he changed sides, helping Henry VI back to the throne. He was killed at the Battle of Barnet.

WORCESTER, THOMAS PERCY, EARL OF (1397 - 1403 b. 1343?) Brother of Henry Percy, 1st Earl of Northumberland and uncle of Hotspur, he served Edward III with distinction, but deserted Richard II in favour of Henry IV. Changing sides again along with the other Percys in 1403, he was taken prisoner after the Battle of Shrewsbury and beheaded.

VANBRUGH, SIR JOHN (1664 - 1726) England's most successful baroque architect. Seaton Delaval Hall, Blenheim Palace and Castle Howard are claimed to be his finest pieces.

VORTIGERN, KING OF THE BRITONS. The word vortigern means 'over-king' and was the nickname given to a Romano-British nobleman. His employment of Anglo-Saxon mercenaries enabled him to control most of Britain from around 425 onwards. Eventually he lost control of the mercenaries, despite huge grants of land and (possibly) marrying the daughter of their leader, Hengest and died in disgrace circa 460.